# Shareplicity 2

## A guide to investing in
## US stock markets

# DANIELLE ECUYER

First published in 2021 by Major Street Publishing Pty Ltd
PO Box 106, Highett, Vic. 3190
E | info@majorstreet.com.au  W | majorstreet.com.au  M | +61 421 707 983

A catalogue record for this
book is available from the
National Library of Australia

NATIONAL LIBRARY OF AUSTRALIA

Printed book ISBN: 978-0-6489804-6-9
Ebook ISBN: 978-0-6489804-7-6

Cover design by Peter Reardon
Internal design by Production Works
Printed in Australia by Ovato, an Accredited ISO AS/NZS 14001:2004
Environmental Management System Printer.

10 9 8 7 6 5 4 3 2 1

# Praise for *Shareplicity 2*

'Danielle Ecuyer's *Shareplicity 2* is a clear and easily understood explanation of what drives share market valuations and how she sees the future of share investing.

'It is based on the simple and compelling proposition that we live in a time of incredible technological change, innovation and disruption, greatly accelerated by the pandemic, and that a lot of the big innovative companies riding the wave of the future are based in the US or listed on stock exchanges there, or form part of many major ETFs. Therefore, if you want to invest successfully and ride the wave of disruption and growth, you need to invest there either directly in shares or through ETFs and equivalent assets in the US.

'Danielle describes the investment landscape clearly and compellingly, and argues her case well. She does not write in a dry and academic tone. You can imagine you are sitting in a room with her talking to you directly.

'For anyone interested in investment, who wants to understand the markets and what drives them, and how to embark on the task of investing yourself (rather than through advisers or fund managers), this is a really worthwhile book.

'Danielle gives readers the confidence and the toolkit to create a sense of their own agency through having a deeper understanding of investment, the markets and how they all work.'

**Lucy Hughes Turnbull AO**

'Technology has made it easier than ever to invest overseas, and Danielle's book is the essential guide for all Australians on investing in the world's biggest stock markets.'

**Equity Mates**

'I've been an investor my whole life and have guided my investments in the belief that two of America's greatest assets are its technology and innovation. Throughout my career, identifying the companies and trends in technology, and the industries where technology can cause disruption and opportunity, has been the key to building wealth from investing in US stocks.

'Often, investors and academics today are weighed down by concepts and economic philosophies of the past, and their analysis is flawed by these biases. It is refreshing to find a book that accurately gives investors real insights into investing in technology and innovation in the US markets.

'If you like making money in stocks, *Shareplicity 2* will serve you well. Much of the book covers key ideas for furthering the understanding of which stocks and trends will drive stock prices upward and why. I find myself often in debate with investors wedded to fundamental concepts of economics or stock analysis, yet the world and the way companies are valued has adapted to the changes in society driven by technology. In fact, change happens faster today than ever, providing opportunities to investors who are able to identify these trends and companies that will best capitalize from them.

'*Shareplicity 2* breaks down the fundamental concepts and changes in the modern markets and systems that many investing books fail to understand or articulate. It also gives investors the fundamentals and facts behind the modern market thinking and valuations. *Shareplicity 2* is certainly a great take for investors who want to understand current US markets and, most of all, make money investing in the future.'

**Ross Gerber, President and CEO, Gerber Kawasaki, Inc.**

'In the heady days of meme stocks, online forums, FOMO and TINA, *Shareplicity 2* is a refreshing introduction to the real world of investing in US companies (and it also includes an acronym or two!).

'Taking a dive into megatrends, risk versus reward and strategy, *Shareplicity 2* walks readers through the macro influences that will make or break future performance while detailing what should form the foundations of every US share portfolio.

'By referencing other big minds, Danielle Ecuyer empowers investors to take their own journey to investing in the US; she doesn't tell readers what stocks to buy, though she unabashedly advocates for investing in future-focused companies and explains why.

'Readers of *Shareplicity 2* will come away with a deeper understanding of how US markets work, why companies are worth what they are (or aren't!) and how to avoid losing money. Readers should find it easy to put their newly acquired knowledge to good use.

'Danielle Ecuyer's insights are a calm inner voice investors can draw on as they navigate the crosscurrents of investing in the US during these unprecedented times, and with interest rates on the cusp of changing course.'

**Nadine Blayney, Head of Content/Anchor, ausbiz**


'Investing in the US stock market creates diversity in your share portfolio. It offers access to far more themes and opportunities than are available in any other markets in the world, and which dwarf the opportunities available in Australia. Danielle starts with the macro picture and then eloquently weaves an easy-to-read and hard-to-put-down narrative on how to capitalise on current big-picture themes and sectors and, in particular, the secular megatrends that are changing our world.'

**Vic Jokovic, CEO, Chi-X Funds**

# Contents

# 1

## Ford versus Tesla

### The movie

It is Hollywood's grandest night on the film calendar, the Oscars. There is so much excitement around the latest blockbuster from the Netflix stable, *Ford versus Tesla*.

The all-star cast is headed by Christian Bale who plays the enigmatic engineering genius Elon Musk. Rumour has it that this is one of Bale's best performances, and the buzz is electric as the media and crowds wait for Bale and Musk to arrive in the latest self-driving Model S Plaid.

Netflix jumped at the opportunity to produce and distribute this David versus Goliath story of Mr Musk's sustainable energy and transport company, which saved the world from climate catastrophe despite the legacy giants of the 20th century – oil and the internal combustion engine (ICE) companies, as represented by the Ford Motor Company.

The tale covers the 30-year struggle and eventual victory of Tesla corporation to accelerate the world's move to mass transport with electric vehicles (EVs), autonomous robotaxi fleets, semi-trailers and renewable energy systems and battery storage.

The almost cult-like, religious following Musk and Bale have means the Twittersphere is alight with anticipation of the awards ceremony, which is being live-streamed across the globe.

'STOP! Hold it right there!'

'What's all this talk about a new Netflix film?' you ask. 'Danielle has lost the plot! There is no movie; there is no victory; there is no way one man and his vision can disrupt the US$11 trillion automotive and oil markets; it's just not possible!'

## The reality

Yes, you are right, there is no movie – yet. And the story, while 20 years in the making, is only just gathering momentum.

Now, before you become concerned that this chapter and the book are just a promotion for Tesla, I want you to take a deep breath and possibly a leap of readerly faith, and continue reading. As you will discover, the story is in the early stages, but it represents one of the most profound disruptive changes you and I will live through.

The story is equally important for appreciating the winds of changes blowing through the US stock markets and how you can invest to make the most of all the differing dynamics of the largest stock indices in the world.

## Why the Ford versus Tesla story matters

The story of Ford versus Tesla – or any other ICE manufacturer, such as General Motors (GM) or Volkswagen (VW) – is emblematic of the technological disruption and the change the world is experiencing.

Elon Musk's vision to 'accelerate the development of sustainable energy' was rooted in his concern that the world would reach peak oil. (This theory was viewed as probable until fracking became economically viable and the USA once again assumed the title of the world's largest oil producer, with the shale oil discoveries in West Texas, Permian Basin.)

What started as a risk-adjusted strategy to produce EVs to offset declining oil production has transformed into a race to cease the world's fossil-fuel dependence.

While some would frame the EV upstart as David versus the ICE Goliaths, the truth is somewhat different. Suppose the ultimate goal were to accelerate the world's transition to sustainable energy and transport, as stated. In that case, the goal is on the first leg of achievement, given the flood of announcements from major car-manufacturing companies in late 2020 and early 2021 (Ford, GM, VW and Mini among them) that they would transition away from traditional combustion engines to zero emission technologies.

'Tesla's long-term competitive strength will be primarily manufacturing. This is counterintuitive, but I'm quite confident this will be what happens,' Elon Musk was reported as saying in 2020.

## Looking ahead

According to Mr Musk, Tesla will be producing up to 20 million EVs by 2030, up from the 500,000 in production and sales in 2020, and a record first quarter 2021 figure of 185,000. To put that into context, the current leading ICE manufacturers (VW and Toyota) produce around 10 million vehicles annually.

Toyota has around a 10% global market share, followed by VW at approximately 7.5% and then Ford at 5.6%.

Moreover, the current three-year goal is to make the basic Tesla model affordable to the masses, at a price point of US$25,000. With a 400-mile range (around 640 km), this model is pitched at existing popular ICE models, remembering that the ongoing running costs of an EV are lower than those of existing ICE fleets.

The EV industry could be more transformative than most people envisage, due to potential deflationary forces that would make traditional combustion engines just too expensive to manufacture. It is probably too challenging for most of you to grasp such a change now, but combustion engine vehicles are far more complex to manufacture, and they have many more moving parts and components than an EV. So, with the technological advances, the proposition that EVs will displace ICE mobility is not that farfetched.

Tesla has become the catalyst, with its single model roadster produced in 2010, and its public listing at $17 per share giving it a US$1.7 billion market capitalisation.

At US$650 per share in March 2021, post a 5-for-1 share split or US$3,250 pre-split, Tesla has a market capitalisation of some US$650 billion. The value ascribed to the stock is bewildering to most experts and traditional investors. Trading on a price-to-earnings (PER) multiple of over 150x 2021 earnings, it cannot be described as cheap (more about PERs in Chapters 4, 8 and 9). Despite what the market narrative may signal, value is often in the eye of the beholder.

For the diehard investors and fans, Tesla remains undervalued relative to the future earnings growth that they believe is probable. One estimate suggests Tesla could become a US$1 trillion revenue company by 2030, compared to forecast revenue of some US$53 billion in 2021, with the current EV production targets and other ancillary battery, solar and software services for autonomous or self-driving vehicles in the works too. Envisage the concept of a smart car with multiple software services, such as downloadable wireless upgrades of gaming and entertainment features as well as FSD (full self-driving) software. (Apple has achieved the same by taking the hardware of your smart phone and other Mac products and providing software and streaming services through Apple TV and its App Store.) Some analysts have calculated that Tesla's annual revenue can compound at up to a 50% growth rate this decade.

The biggest problem the company currently faces is meeting demand for the EVs while being able to sustainably scale manufacturing capacity within cashflow and funding constraints. As I write, the company is building two new giga factories in Texas and Berlin and expanding its Shanghai giga factory. Another factory in England has been mooted by the media and India is mentioned regularly as displaying some interest in working with Tesla.

There have been more than a few speed humps on the Tesla stockholder journey, including significant production problems with the Model 3 in early 2019; a Twitter storm between Mr Musk and the Securities and Exchange Commission (SEC), and the ongoing battle between the naysayers, short sellers and Mr Musk.

In spite of the eccentric nature of Tesla's CEO, his genius and ability to succeed were evidenced in 2020, when the company achieved the goal of almost 500,000 EV production and sales in a year of lockdown disruption and a pandemic.

In 2020, the Tesla stock price was rerated and included in the S&P 500 index. Some experts have described the success as the weaponisation of the stock price, meaning the demand for the stock at such elevated price levels allowed Tesla to raise billions in cash at very cheap valuations.

The company has some US$19 billion in cash at its disposal and with each new giga factory priced at around US$1 billion, it is hardly surprising those investors with a long-term view accept the proposition that the goal to achieve the 20 million EV production rate by 2030 is possible if not probable. Of course, execution risk remains high, but at least Tesla is not encumbered with old legacy factories that need retrofitting.

## Arch rival Ford

This is where we segue to the Ford Motor Company, which is not without controversy either. It might be one of the most famous global brands, and bear the surname of the founding father of mass-produced automobiles, but its journey has been far from wealth-creating.

Ford's loss-making overseas expansion efforts and an overly indebted balance sheet have created a world of pain for investors over many years, culminating in the collapse in demand for new motor vehicles and trucks in 2020. From a high of some US$37 in 1997, the stock traded below US$4 in 2020.

A new CEO, James Farley (formerly COO or Chief Operating Officer), who took the reins at the beginning of October 2020, has committed to reorienting the company away from the traditional combustion engines to electric vehicles and autonomous cars.

Ford aims to invest US$29 billion in electric and self-driving technology through to 2025. It has recently launched the electric Ford Mustang Mach-E and redesigned the best-selling F-150 truck. The company is also relaunching an old favourite, the Ford Bronco.

Investors have taken heart from the strategic shift and, combined with the expected post-pandemic pick-up in the US economy, the Ford stock price has risen like the tide to a 52-week high of US$13 on 15 March 2021. But, even with the rerating, Ford's valuation pales into insignificance at 11x 2021 earnings compared to Tesla's eye-watering 150x.

Even though 2021 marked the watershed year that started the global transition to zero-emission mobility, the transition will be littered with winning and losing stocks along the way.

Ford is emblematic of one of the many major incumbent ICE manufacturers either starting or accelerating on the transition journey, which has coincided fortuitously with a dramatic uptick in economic demand post the pandemic.

Tesla, on the other hand, is just one of the many new EV manufacturers that are evolving in response to expected future demand for zero-emissions vehicles.

Equally, these two companies go to the heart of some of the most debated metrics and investing styles in the US stock markets – value versus growth, or the older DNA cyclical, often termed value stocks (Ford) and the newer DNA stocks (Tesla, NIO and Rivian), in some instances growth stocks, changing the world through innovative technological disruption.

The argument is that growth stocks have been supported over the last decade by lower-for-longer interest rates. Now the tide is turning, with a potential major cyclical uptrend in inflation, and the strongest economic growth since World War 2, post the 2020 depression-like recessions.

Here lies the problem for investors: how can you navigate the big picture macro-economic trends of rising interest rates and rising economic growth against the potentially accelerating impact of technological change? And how will valuations for these stocks change over time?

The example of the fictitious *Ford versus Tesla* movie is symbolic of the rate and speed of technological change that is cutting across every aspect of our lives. Investors face huge challenges when trying to assess whether it is more advantageous to buy the cheaper, older, value stocks such as Ford or back the new company that is potentially changing the world.

Not since Henry Ford began the mass production of his Model T has anyone attempted to transform two of the world's largest industries – energy (oil and renewables) and automobiles (and trucks and semi-trailers) – with new technology, batteries. And no, we are not talking about the Eveready 'bunny' batteries!

Much of Ford's success was achieved when the company was privately owned. It wasn't until 1956, when the company went public, that management had to deal with the demands of stockholders.

Elon Musk, by comparison, has to finely balance the strategic demands and mission of the company with delivering profits to stockholders. One without the other means the value proposition may fail.

Ford and other legacy manufacturers are battling the demons of disruption. (A similar impact was made by the Japanese car manufacturers on the US automotive industry from the late 1970s onwards.) Their challenge is to transition existing factories into new ones, invest in the change and at the same time disrupt the existing bestsellers.

## Why invest in the US?

Ford versus Tesla is one example of the old versus the new. The story could have easily been Verizon or AT&T versus Apple, Walmart versus Amazon or Disney versus Netflix. This is where you make the money: if you had seen the potential of Amazon, Netflix or Facebook, you would be sitting pretty. The US has driven global technological change over the last 50 years, and the rest of the world has followed. If this trend is to continue, then Australian investors have to learn how to invest in US stocks.

If I were to give a one-word answer to why I invest in US stocks, the word would be 'innovation' – plain and simple. The US stock markets are not only the largest in the world but they offer investment opportunities in some of the best and most innovative companies.

Of course, the Australian and other developed stock markets, such as those in Europe and Japan, have relevance, but as you will learn, time and again, diversification and risk management are key to growing your wealth over the long term.

Although some investors are giving up on the US and turning their focus to China and other emerging markets, I believe the US stock markets will continue to play a major role for investors and offer excellent money-making opportunities this decade.

The pandemic has ironically given rise to an acceleration in technological innovation, and the macro-economic responses to the 2020 recession are creating a forecast uptick in economic activity not seen since the end of the World War 2. The combination of these two factors creates a 'Goldilocks' backdrop for investors, (an economy that is growing without over-heating and posing inflationary threats), as long as you are equipped with the necessary information to break down and assess the opportunities in the US stock markets.

*Shareplicity 2* has been written to help anyone who seeks a greater understanding of how to successfully invest in the US. While you may not completely appreciate the subtleties at this stage, this book will guide you through how US stock markets have evolved to where they are post pandemic and what lies ahead.

Ford and Tesla are the symbolic microcosm of the world of US investing that I am going to introduce you to.

*Shareplicity 2* is a guide to help you understand how to invest profitably in the US stock markets, and it also aims to deliver you comprehensive coverage and analysis of the biggest debates and investment themes that are set to continue to dominate investing over the next decade.

Chapter 2, 'US stock markets and the major indices', starts your journey with an explanation of the different stock markets, indices and what they mean for the way in which you can invest. Chapter 3, 'The US now and into the future', dives into how the macro-economic themes have evolved over the last 40 years and how that has potentially shaped the big picture for investors for the future. Don't worry if this is sounding too complex: I dissect the issues and explain them in terms that are easy to understand.

In Chapter 4, 'Valuing the top 20 US giants', you learn about the largest 20 companies in the US and how investors can value the stocks. The walk through the giants will help you on the pathway to understanding the difference between the investing narratives of value and growth, and how the macro-economic big picture can impact on what themes or trends the investing community gravitates towards.

Chapters 5 and 6 take a good, hard look at secular trends and, in particular, the major megatrends and the companies in those sectors that have the potential to mint millionaires over the next decade.

Chapter 7 examines the financial products referred to as 'exchange traded funds' (ETFs) and explores the various avenues through which you can invest in the US (and other overseas markets for that matter) via ETFs. The burgeoning investing style of screening companies based on environmental, social and governance (ESG) criteria is shaping both companies and strategic stock-picking as well as the composition of ETFs in the third decade of the 21st century, and you will learn all about these measures and how they are employed by investors.

With all this new information, I guide you through constructing US stock portfolios in Chapter 8. This chapter looks at how to manage volatility and create baskets of stocks, and I give an overview of all the US sectors in the S&P 500 to help you understand how to asset-allocate across stocks, sectors and themes.

Chapter 9 moves on to discuss some interesting titbits that you need to know to enhance and expand your investing experience. This chapter tackles the differences between valuation metrics and how they are relevant to different types of companies, as well as some unique research into how central bank liquidity and new investment products may be impacting stocks.

All this information is wrapped up in some final thoughts for you to take away with your newfound knowledge of US stock markets at the precipice of technological innovation and change.

There are many different ways and routes to invest in the US stock markets: from differing factors such as value versus growth or old versus new economy stocks; how to manage sectors and themes; and how important the interest rate and inflation narratives potentially are on the way in which stocks, sectors and themes move in and out of favour.

Therefore, as is always the case, you need to assess your own situation and risk tolerance. Before you can invest effectively, it's important to understand what you are trying to achieve, your timescales and how well you tolerate volatile movements in stock prices.

The mantra for *Shareplicity 2* is this: we can't control the stock markets, but we can control how we respond. Knowledge is powerful, as accessing the best information will hopefully allow you to make better and more informed investing decisions. Buying stocks is not about being an expert or being right all the time. Investing is about knowing where to access expert information and how to interpret it to your benefit.

While some of the preliminary information in the early chapters may seem unnecessary, it aims to provide you with a solid base of understanding upon which to make your investing decisions. Many of us like to take the simplest and easiest route, but the US stock market has a habit of reminding us who is boss when we become too *laissez-faire* and don't spend the time understanding our investing goals and how we will achieve them.

As you read the book, remember that investing in stocks is very personal and everyone will develop the pathways that suit them best. I do hope you enjoy the next phase of the Shareplicity journey. For new readers, I hope you take away some insights that you may not have been aware of.

Let the US journey begin!

# 2

# US stock markets and the major indices

Accessibility to investing in global stock markets has been made possible through the internet, innovation and competitive pressures. The internet and increased competition from overseas low-cost trading platforms have opened up opportunities for average investors. The disruption evident across so many industries has played a part in allowing people like me and you to invest internationally from anywhere – even on a smart phone, sometimes with zero transaction fees! The shift to looking overseas for investment opportunities has also been driven in part by lower-than-average returns, until recently, from traditional Aussie favourites like the banks and oil and gas (energy) companies since 2015.

The demographic of investors is changing too. More millennial and gen Z investors are seeking to profit from some of the big technology names that frame their lifestyles.

So, our focus in this book is on how to invest, understand and analyse the largest stock markets in the world – those portrayed by so many stories and Hollywood films set around Wall Street.

The USA is not only home to the world's largest and most successful companies, it also continues to dominate the world stage with the size of its stock markets. One US stock, Apple, has a market capitalisation over US$2 trillion; the entire Australian share market has a market capitalisation of around US$1.5 trillion. It is not unusual for global behemoths like Apple or Amazon to have a size (market capitalisation) in excess of a country's entire stock exchange.

There is a generally accepted rule of thumb that goes like this: the US stock markets are the dog that wags the tail for other developed markets, such as Australia. This means most world markets tend, on average, to follow the trend set by the US stock markets.

To understand the US markets, however, we must see them in context.

## Developed (mature) and developing (emerging) markets

The US is classified as a developed (or mature) market. Other developed markets include Australia, Canada, the UK, Europe and Japan. 'Developed' stock markets are those where the underlying economies are mature: they usually have lower levels of economic growth but a well-developed middle class and aging populations.

Developing (or emerging) markets are newer economies that are embracing more Western cultures. As the lower-income class is moving to the more affluent middle class, the economic growth of the country is typically higher than in the developed markets. Per capita income is normally lower than in developed countries, but the expectation is for the emerging middle class to grow their wealth and per capita income to reach or exceed the standards of developed countries.

China is, of course, the largest economy and market that is considered emerging. Following in its wake are Korea, Taiwan,

Thailand, India, Indonesia, the Philippines and Vietnam, for example. Other emerging markets across the globe include Brazil, Argentina, Chile, Mexico, Russia, Turkey, Saudi Arabia, Qatar, the UAE and South Africa, in no particular order.

The list of countries currently considered to be emerging markets can be found in the Morgan Stanley Country Index (MSCI).

The index may have 1292 constituents, but China represents 42.24% of the index, followed by Taiwan (12.67%), South Korea (11.9%), India (8.15%) and Brazil (4.39%).

## Why emerging markets are relevant

Before you worry that I have gone off course, I want to highlight that when discussing the US stock markets, we need to keep an eye on what the large emerging markets – especially China – are doing. With so much interdependence and friction over trade and technology between the world's two largest powers – the USA and China – investors should remain in tune with potential changing dynamics.

As much as we might think it's different in other markets, from a macro perspective many of the secular themes (which we'll discuss further in Chapters 5 and 6) that investors witness in their domestic stock market are also playing out in other stock markets, because many of the large companies driving the change are global anyway.

We are part of a global investing world, and that interconnectivity feeds into the way stock prices move when interest rates and currency levels change.

Emerging markets tend to perform more strongly when there is a weaker US dollar. This is because many of these countries – and the companies listed on their stock exchanges – hold

US-dollar-denominated debt. If the US dollar rises, it costs the country more in its domestic currency to service the interest payments or pay off the debt. Conversely, a weaker US dollar is beneficial to servicing the debt costs. Emerging markets also benefit during periods of economic expansion, such as the world is experiencing in 2021 after the pandemic recession.

What's happening in China – the world's largest emerging market – is, of course, extremely important for investors in the US stock markets. In *Shareplicity 2*, we view the ascension of China through the prism of how it impacts US stocks.

## Stock exchanges, markets and indices

I understand why investors' eyes glaze over when I'm discussing the difference between a stock exchange, a market and an index, but it's necessary to make the distinctions between the three.

Put as simply as possible:

- ► The **stock exchange** is the infrastructure that supports the market where the exchange (sale and purchase) of stocks takes place.

- ► The **market** is a term loosely used to describe the stocks (shares) that are listed and traded on the exchange.

- ► An **index** represents the collective price movements of a designated group of stocks. The stocks that make up the index are included based on different criteria. The most common criterion is a market capitalisation weight, market capitalisation being the number of shares on issue multiplied by the share price.

### US stock exchanges and markets

There are three main places to trade US stocks:

1. **The New York Stock Exchange** (NYSE) is the largest stock exchange in the world and is valued at over US$24 trillion. It is located at 11 Wall Street in New York City and was founded in 1792. There are some 2400 companies listed on the NYSE, and the stocks are traded through an auction between the buyers and the sellers. The NYSE trades stocks included in all major indices: the Dow Jones, the S&P 500 and the Russell indices (1000, 2000 and 3000).

2. **The Nasdaq** does not have a physical location. It is referred to as a dealer's market, where the stocks are traded digitally through market makers or dealers, as opposed to directly between buyers and sellers. The Nasdaq is the second largest stock market after the NYSE and is valued at around US$19 trillion.

3. **OTC** refers to 'over the counter'. Specific companies that specialise in OTC traded stocks will make a market in those companies that are traded but not listed on a specific exchange. OTC stocks are bought and sold through market makers.

## The rest of the world

To give this some context, let's look at the rest of the world.

In descending order and quoted in US dollars, the Shanghai stock exchange is valued at US$6.5 trillion, Hong Kong at $6.48 trillion, Japan $6.35 trillion, Shenzhen at $4.9 trillion, Euronext (Belgium, France, Italy, Netherlands, Norway and Portugal) $US4.88 trillion and LSE Group (UK) at US$3.67 trillion. Australia comes in at sixteenth, valued at around US$1.53 trillion.

Of course, these numbers will vary depending on stock price movements and the value of the US dollar relative to the currency of the stock exchange. (These valuations are as at 21 January 2021 from Statistica.)

## US stock indices

There are some 3500 stocks listed in the US, and many are included in several indices. The number will vary depending upon what criteria are assumed, such as whether the company is US domiciled or traded on an exchange or OTC. Equally, there is overlap between different indices; Apple and Microsoft are two examples of stocks that are included in all three major indices.

The three most well-known and discussed indices are the Dow Jones Industrial Average (DIJA), the S&P 500 and the Nasdaq 100. There are also the Russell 1000, 2000 and 3000 indices and a list of sectoral indices as described by Standard & Poor's. The most all-encompassing index of all investible and traded publicly listed companies in the US is known as the Wilshire 5000.

Looking at the indices separately allows you to ascertain the different companies represented. Due to the size and choice of stocks listed in the US, even new investors ought to understand which underlying companies are represented in an index.

Each index trades differently depending on the stocks it includes, the weighting of each stock in the index, which sector and industries the stocks represent, and whether the index has a greater domestic or international slant. Choosing an index to invest in is a bit like going to the cheese counter at your supermarket and trying to decide which cheese fits all your needs (the cheese counter is the index, and the different cheeses are the stocks). Is it good value and at the right price point? Is it suitable to eat on crackers, or best used in cooking? If I am averse to cholesterol, does it meet my nutritional needs? If I want to avoid dairy, is it vegan?

The indices are not all the same: each has individual characteristics or personalities, trading patterns and influences, so to talk about 'buying the US stock market' is too simplistic.

It is also important that you understand the constituents of an index when you purchase passively managed ETF products that track the index (more about this in Chapters 7 and 8, when we examine some of the largest stocks in the US and in which sectors and indices they reside).

Now, let's look at some of the most notable indices in turn to shed some light on their structure and composition. You don't need to become an index expert, but an in-theory understanding should allow you to improve your decision-making when investing in actively managed funds or ETFs or directly in the US. It will also help you understand why some indices move or perform differently to others.

## The Dow Jones Industrial Average

The Dow Jones Industrial Average (DJIA) – also referred to as the Dow – is unusual as it weights the top 30 US stocks by price rather than market capitalisation.

The top 30 shares usually represent some of the largest US 'blue chips'. The inclusion of the word 'industrial' in the index's name is a hangover from the name given to the index by its founder, Charles Dow, in 1896; most of the stocks in the DJIA are no longer classified as 'industrial'.

As there are only 30 shares in the index, the index's movements are often related to the change in the share price of one or two stocks. The lower the number of stocks in an index, the greater the influence of each stock price.

The DJIA was valued at around US$8 trillion at the end of the September 2020 quarter.

Here is the composition at the time of writing, in alphabetical order: 3M, American Express, Amgen, Apple, Boeing, Caterpillar, Chevron, Cisco, Coca-Cola, Disney, Dow, Goldman Sachs, Home Depot, Honeywell, IBM, Intel, Johnson & Johnson,

JPMorgan Chase, McDonald's, Merck, Microsoft, Nike, Procter & Gamble, Salesforce, Travellers, UnitedHealth Group, Verizon, Visa, Walgreens Boots Alliance and Walmart.

The index was most recently adjusted to reflect Apple's four-for-one share split, meaning shareholders received four shares for every one they held prior to the ex-date of 27 August 2020. The split consequently reduced the price of Apple shares, so the index had to reflect the change in the Apple share price.

In another recent adjustment, Exxon Mobil was removed from the Dow index and Salesforce was added. Many stock market commentators cited this as a strong example of how the old-world-economy stocks – oil and gas, as represented by Exxon Mobil – are being replaced by the new-world-economy stocks – represented here by Salesforce, one of the world's largest software companies.

## The S&P 500

The Standard & Poor's 500 – or S&P 500, as it is usually referred to – was created in 1962 and is an index of the 500 major stocks from the leading industries in 11 sectors: Energy, Materials, Industrials, Consumer Discretionary, Consumer Staples, Health Care, Financials, Information Technology, Communication Services, Real Estate and Utilities. (Sectors are explained in more detail in Chapter 8.)

The stocks included are not necessarily the largest from each sector. Instead, each stock is weighted by market capitalisation and selected on a number of criteria. As stated at spglobal.com:

'To be eligible for S&P 500 index inclusion, a company should be a U.S. company, have a market capitalization of at least USD 8.2 billion, be highly liquid, have a public float of at least 50% of its shares outstanding, and its most recent quarter's earnings and the sum of its trailing four consecutive quarters' earnings must be positive.'

The S&P 500 represents over 83% of the total US equity market capitalisation and thus is a good index to capture the majority of companies listed in the US, as well as being a good representation of the US economy.

The most controversial inclusion (on 21 December 2020) is Tesla. The electric vehicle (EV), battery and solar panel manufacturer is controversial because it is the largest inclusion ever made into the S&P 500, with an over $400 billion market capitalisation. It is not only the size of the company that's notable but also the relatively small free float (the shares that are free to trade daily and not locked away in the hands of major shareholders like Elon Musk).

## The Nasdaq 100

The Nasdaq 100 is a market-capitalisation-weighted index of the largest *non-financial* companies listed on the Nasdaq stock market. It comprises predominantly technology stocks – though it also includes health care and biotechnology stocks – and includes companies from outside the USA. The top ten stocks represent around 50% of the Nasdaq, and which companies they are should come as little surprise: as at 5 March 2021, the top ten by market capitalisation were, in order, Apple, Microsoft, Amazon, Facebook, Alphabet (Google's parent company), Tesla, Facebook, Nvidia, PayPal, Netflix and Comcast.

Did you see I highlighted non-financial companies earlier?

Although many people see the Nasdaq as the technology index, due to the large weighting of tech stocks, it is better to think of it as simply being devoid of the old-economy or value/cyclical stocks such as the banks and insurance companies. Technology stocks represent 57% of the total weight of the Nasdaq 100 versus 20% of the S&P 500, as at the end March 2020 after the COVID-19 stock market crash.

Looking at the long-term performance of the two indices, the Nasdaq 100 produced a total return (capital gain and dividend income) of 608% between 31 December 2007 and 31 December 2020, while the total return of the S&P 500 over the same period was 236%. This represents an annualised return for the Nasdaq 100 of 16.2% versus 9.8% for the S&P 500.

## The Russell indices: Russell 1000, 2000 and 3000

The Russell indices were created by Frank Russell in 1984 and are managed by FTSE Russell, a subsidiary of the London Stock Exchange.

- ► Russell 3000 aims to represent the entire US stock market, with 3000 constituents weighted by market capitalisation.
- ► Russell 2000 is a subset of the 3000 and represents the smallest 2000 companies listed. This index is weighted by market capitalisation and free-float adjusted (meaning only the shares available to investors are included, not the shares tightly held by majority shareholders, for example) for the 2000 smallest listed US companies, and represents 10% of the value of the Russell 3000.
- ► Russell 1000 represents the largest 1000 listed on the US exchanges.

The Russell 2000 is often perceived as the best measure or indicator of how the US economy – and small businesses in particular – are doing, as the larger indices are often distorted by the major companies such as Amazon, Apple and Microsoft.

The constituents of the Russell indices are traded on the NYSE, the Nasdaq and OTC.

## The Wilshire 5000 Total Market Index

The Wilshire 5000 was created in 1974 to represent the 5000 publicly listed companies in the USA. The index grew to over 7500 in mid-1998 in the evolving dotcom (tech and telecom) boom and has since shrunk to around 3500. The tide may be turning in late 2020 and 2021 with the stream of new company listings – often called IPOs (initial public offerings) and special purpose acquisition companies (SPACs).

The index is weighted by market capitalisation and only includes companies that are headquartered in the USA, are publicly traded on a US stock exchange and which have stock pricing readily available.

## The volatility index

The volatility index (VIX) was created by the Chicago Board Options Exchange (CBOE) and is often referred to as the 'fear gauge', or 'fear index', for stocks. The VIX represents a live index of the expectations of movements in the S&P 500 in the near term and is calculated from the short-dated future options on the S&P 500. In lay speak, it's a price indicator of where the options market expects the S&P to trade in the near term.

Investors focus on the VIX as it provides a potential indication of where the US share markets will go. The two generally move in the opposite direction: as the VIX index rises, stock prices fall; when the VIX falls, stock prices rise.

As a general rule, the Nasdaq 100 is the most volatile of the three main indices; that is, its stock prices move up and down more sharply, due to the heavy technology weighting. The Dow Jones is typically the least volatile, and the S&P 500 is somewhere in between.

Did you know you can buy an ETF that tracks volatility? The ticker code is VIXY in the US. Although some advisers may recommend you buy this ETF as protection for possible future stock market sell-offs, from personal experience I would tread carefully. Many of these hedging tools that retail investors can buy have more going on behind the scenes than we are aware of. The VIX and VIXY did spike during the March 2020 sell-off, but once momentum turned, the upward movement reversed swiftly.

From personal experience, playing the VIXY and bear funds (those ETFs that appreciate when stock markets fall) can often compound losses. I discuss these types of ETFs in more detail in Chapter 7; however, I do not see these products as easy risk-management tools for the average investor.

Also, while this book won't go into how quantitative trading and algorithms are executed in the market, you should be aware that hedge funds, for example, have been using the VIX to generate returns. This has been popular and works well – until volatility spikes with an exogenous event such as the pandemic. These kinds of strategies work in the good times, when stock markets are neutral to positive; problems arise when stocks fall. Chapter 9 looks at some of the narratives that are driving the stock markets.

## Other financial instruments for trading stocks

For completeness, I'll quickly run through other financial instruments you may come across.

### American Depository Receipts (ADR)

An ADR or American Depository Receipt is issued by US banks so that US investors can buy overseas companies, including some of Australia's largest companies or well-known foreign companies, such as Nokia, Unilever or Royal Dutch Petroleum.

The ADR can be traded on the NYSE or over the counter (OTC) and is a financial security that represents the underlying stock by a different factor, such as 5 or 10 shares per ADR priced in US dollars. Dividends are paid in US dollars to the investors.

## OTC

OTC trades are those that may require an investor to speak to a dealer, as the orders cannot always be input into a trading platform. Generally, OTC orders are for larger, more sophisticated investors and would allow the purchase of foreign shares on the NYSE or Nasdaq.

### SPACs or blank-cheque companies

Special purpose acquisition companies (SPACs), also referred to as 'blank-cheque companies' (for those readers who are old enough to know what a cheque is!), are listed as an IPO (initial public offering) with no underlying businesses. Instead, the cash is used to buy more embryonic companies from the likes of private equity funds and these are held until the company is publicly listed.

Although SPACs have been around for decades, the huge boost in liquidity from the Federal Reserve and the appetite from retail investors for accessing potential long-term winners pre-IPO have made SPACs very popular.

## The mighty bond market

Although this is a book about US stocks and how to invest in the different companies and indices, it is prudent to acknowledge the elephant in the room when it comes to what moves stock prices.

Political adviser James Carville famously said, 'I used to think that if there was reincarnation, I wanted to come back as the president or the pope or as a .400 baseball hitter. But now

I would like to come back as the bond market. You can intimidate everybody'. This quote is famous not only for the baseball analogy (there hasn't been a .400 hitter in Major League Baseball since 1941) but for its allusion to the size and the power of the bond market to influence other markets, stocks, currencies and metals (such as gold).

The bond market and the shape of the yield curve are very important. However, as you'll see in Chapter 4, the bond market now arguably moves more in step with what the Federal Reserve determines, which in turn can be guided by other markets such as stocks.

The bond market is the government (or 'sovereign') debt that is issued by the U.S. Department of Treasury. In the US, it consists of the US treasuries (bonds) issued; Australian bonds are issued by the Australian Government through the Australian Office of Financial Management (AOFM).

The US government issues different bonds with different durations (which signify when they are due to repay the original amount to the investors who own the bonds), such as 1, 2, 5, 10 and even 30 years, and different interest rates, known as the 'yield', are attached to bonds of different durations. Investors buy the bonds when they are auctioned off to raise money for the government, and the bonds then trade over their duration. The more the bonds are in demand, the more the price of the bonds rises, and the more the yield (or 'coupon') on the bonds decreases. This is similar to the yield on shares: the more investors push up the price of the shares, the more the dividend yield declines, assuming the dividend payment stays the same (which a treasury bond coupon does). The inverse happens when investors sell bonds: the yield on the bond goes up. Intuitively, the lower the yield on the bond, the less the cost for governments to raise money and the lower the cost to borrow for companies.

The International Capital Market Association (ICMA) estimates that the US domestic bond market – defined as the US treasuries and government agencies at national, regional and local levels – is US$22.7 trillion, 91% of which are US treasuries (those issued by the Federal Reserve Bank). Then there is the US corporate bond market, valued around US$10 trillion, with debt maturities as far as 30 years out.

There is also a category of financial instruments called 'treasury inflation protected securities' (TIPS) that are inflation-adjusted bond-like securities. These are not guaranteed by the government and are therefore not as secure or safe from a default perspective. However, institutional investors buy TIPS to protect their income returns from a potential rise in the inflation rate (that is, the consumer price index, or CPI).

I explore the relationship between the bond and stock markets and the US economy – and how this relates to you as an investor – in a lot more depth in Chapter 3.

### Yield curves

I want to touch briefly on the concept of yield curves, as *historically* the direction of the yield curve has been a signal to the stock market about future economic conditions. I emphasise that word because there is an increasing amount of expert literature questioning whether the world will ever see a return to historical precedents in financial markets.

For the moment all you need to understand is the following:

- ► A positive yield curve is traditionally when the bond yield (the interest rate received by investors) is lower at what is called the 'short end' (bonds with shorter durations, such as two years) than at the 'long end' (bonds with longer durations, such as ten years). This infers that interest rates will rise in the future because economic activity and inflation are expected to rise.

► The opposite of a positive yield curve is an inverted yield curve. This is when the yield is lower at the long end than at the short end. This is typically perceived as a harbinger of the central bank having to lower interest rates in the future, and an expectation that economic activity will decline and a recession may be on the horizon.

Stock markets are very sensitive to what bond markets do, and thus you will often see stocks reacting to the movement in the US 10-year treasury. I explain this in a lot more detail throughout the book, when I cover what has been happening in US stock markets.

## Chapter summary

► A stock exchange is a platform to facilitate the trading of stocks.

► An index is a collection of stocks ranked according to different criteria. It can be replicated by an ETF product.

► In the US markets, some stocks overlap indices, so it is important you understand the different constituents of an index.

► The VIX is referred to as the 'fear' index and indicates the level of perceived future volatility in the stock market.

► How the bond market moves and the shape of the yield curve impact on the stock market.

# 3

# The US now and into the future

It might seem unnecessary – I know you are chomping at the bit for some stock ideas – but understanding the big-picture, macro-economic backdrop for investing in US stocks is the key to unlocking the real wealth-makers.

Most experts, usually economists and strategists, offer a macro-economic view and forecast and, irrespective of whether that considered analysis becomes reality, the expectation is enough to move the stock markets and create both investing opportunities and disappointments.

You will be aware of macro-economic forecasts such as those provided by the Reserve Bank of Australia (RBA) or well-known, longstanding economists such as Shane Oliver (AMP) and Bill Evans (Westpac). US investment banks and experts such as Howard Marks or billionaire Ray Dalio often proffer their views and forecasts of how the US economy will evolve and what the Federal Reserve will do.

These expectations or forecasts frame what is referred to as an 'investing narrative', such as the narrative that a 'V-shaped' economic recovery in 2021 will occur post pandemic. These narratives and forecasts are in large part based on historical precedents and can become the major drivers of how stock-picking is conducted. You will be learning a lot more about how this mechanism works in the following chapters.

If, however, the narrative or expectation does not come to pass, then this may offer you opportunities. The fact that the expectations may not become reality allows you to be ahead of the curve when it comes to understanding US stock market dynamics: a famous Wall Street trope is 'buy on rumour and sell on fact'.

This chapter offers you a brief history of how we arrived at the current situation of booming stock markets reaching record highs after the biggest economic recession in over 90 years. It approaches the present US economic big picture from two angles:

1. How did the world's largest economy get to where it is today?
2. How will it move forward, and what are the implications for the US stock markets?

There is an expression that states, 'the US stock market sneezes and the rest of the world catches a cold'. This encapsulates the might of the US market. Since the end of World War 2, the USA has been the dominant economic powerhouse of the world. It has created the world's reserve currency, the US dollar (meaning other central banks hold US dollars). The US dollar is the currency used to price most major commodities, metals and minerals, and international trade is usually settled in US dollars.

The US dollar is traditionally sought out when investors are fearful or there is what is called a 'risk off' event, such as the outbreak of war or a pandemic. The strength of the US economy, and the security that investors know their money is safe and the value of the currency won't collapse, is what gives investors the perception that holding US currency is better than hiding their savings under the mattress in their domestic currency. For over 70 years, the world has viewed the US government and its financial institutions and currency as unshakeable, reliable and secure.

The hegemony of the USA is increasingly a point of conjecture, however, with the rise of China as a global superpower. While this book does not tackle the potential shifting sands of world power between the incumbent USA and the emerging behemoth China, I think we should assume that the narrative surrounding these two giants is not going away. Readers should be aware that US stocks, like Australian stocks, are sensitive to the changing dynamics of China's situation.

## Setting the stage

Our story arguably starts in 1971, when President Nixon disbanded the Bretton Woods system. Named after the area of Bretton Woods in New Hampshire, USA, the Bretton Woods agreement formed part of the new world order that was created towards the end of World War 2. The agreement replaced the gold standard in 1944 and made the US dollar the dominant world currency (as noted earlier, the reserve currency for trading goods and services).

The Bretton Woods system relied on many countries fixing their currencies to the greenback via the gold price. This, in turn, gave currency markets and foreign currencies rigidity, undermining the ability of central banks to use their own currency as a release valve for changing economic situations (a falling domestic currency supports economic growth).

The system lasted for almost 30 years. However, the rigidity of pegging currencies to the US dollar and gold price caused problems. The dismantling of the Bretton Woods system in 1971 meant other major currencies pegged to the US dollar, such as the then British pound and French franc, were no longer bound by the restrictions. The resulting new floating currencies, such as we have now, began a new era of international trade and interconnectedness, accelerating globalisation, deregulation and international free trade. The early seventies also marked the start of the computer information age.

However, as often happens, the newfound economic and trade freedoms didn't get off to a great start. Two oil-price shocks and strong unionised labour forces helped push inflation to record highs, which in turn led to economic recessions and high unemployment. If the 1950s and 1960s were the boom period post–World War 2, then the 1970s was the dark decade. From a low of 1% in 1965, inflation rose to as high as 14% in 1980. Unemployment in the USA grew from an annual average low of 3.5% in 1969 to 9.7% in 1982.

Little did the experts realise that the solution to the high inflation rates would change the USA's – and the world's – economic trajectory.

## The 1980s ushered in a new era

In 1979, the new chair of the Federal Reserve, Paul Volcker, enters our story. Without fear, he hiked up interest rates to eye-watering levels. US interest rates reached a peak of 20% in June 1981, before falling to 3% in 1983.

If you happen to have watched the Netflix series *The Crown*, series four shows how controversial such a move was, when the newly elected Prime Minister Margaret Thatcher adopted the same inflation-beating policy. Australia followed suit. However, Volcker's policy worked to eradicate the inflation problem, and similar policies that were adopted in Australia and the UK worked too, no matter how politically unpalatable it was at the time.

The accepted wisdom is that overly high or low inflation is not good for our economic prosperity. Central banks – including the Federal Reserve, generally speaking – target an inflation rate of around 2 to 3%.

To offer you some perspective, Figure 1 depicts the historic US inflation. The higher the lines above the horizontal x-axis, the higher the inflation level; the lines below the horizontal line depict deflation. As you can see, inflation peaked in the 1970s before starting a downward march to current levels.

**FIGURE 1: Historic US inflation rates (1950-2020)**

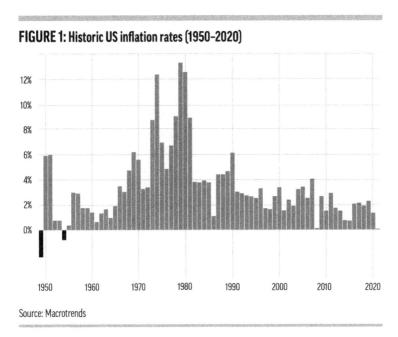

Source: Macrotrends

## Inflation

Before we progress further, we need to pause and reflect on the term 'inflation'. It is one of the most used terms in finance and, like most jargon, it needs some explanation. It is also cited as the main driver of whether interest rates go up or down and has essentially been one of the most important financial indicators for central bank policy – so it's worth understanding.

In my research, I came upon some excellent analysis from Lyn Alden Schwartzer, who runs a very informative online newsletter service. She defines three types of inflation, each with a different driver and influence on the US economy and investing:

1. **Monetary inflation:** Put simply, monetary inflation refers to the increase in money supply, what economists call 'M2'. It includes all cash, notes in circulation and bank deposits. When M2 money supply increases, it means there is just more money in the system.

    Supply is created by banks and financial institutions lending more or, as happened in 2020, the Federal Reserve injecting more liquidity (money) into the system, often called 'QE' or 'quantitative easing'. It is best not to become too bogged down with the different money supply categories, as your target is not to be an economist but a better investor.

2. **Asset price inflation:** This naturally refers to the increase in asset prices – think stocks, property, gold, collectables and even Bitcoin.

3. **Consumer price inflation:** This is the inflation rate most commonly referred to in the investing world. It is measured by the consumer price index (CPI) – the basket of goods and services that all central banks track to establish whether consumer prices are rising or falling. It has historically been, if you recall, the key driver of monetary policy (through the setting of interest rates).

The differences between these types of inflation are illustrated throughout this book.

## Did the 1980s change our world forever?

Going back to Mr Volcker, I want you keep in mind that his main aim was to quash the high levels of consumer price inflation. However, he is only one part of the unwinding story.

As Figure 1 showed, inflation has been trending down from its peak in 1980. Correspondingly, interest rates have also been trending down. This is no coincidence, but the two are not necessarily directly correlated.

Let's take a look at what I mean by that. Going back to big-picture economics, the federal funds rate (or 'cash rate') has continued to decline. US 10-year treasury bonds are a good indicator of interest rate trends and have followed the downward trend, as shown in Figure 2.

**FIGURE 2: US 10-year treasury bonds (1960–2020)**

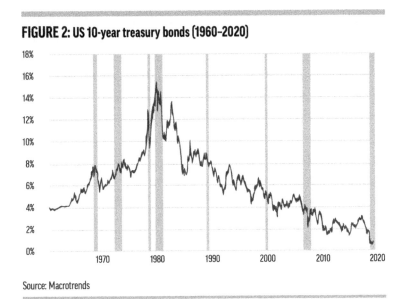

Source: Macrotrends

If we had bought 10-year treasury bonds at the time of issue (when the Federal Reserve sold the bonds), we would have received an interest rate payment equivalent to the percentage number shown on the vertical axis of the chart that aligned with our position on the yield line.

What is most interesting, though, are the vertical grey lines that reflect US recessions (defined as two quarters of negative gross domestic product (GDP) growth in the US). You do not need an economics degree to see that every time a recession starts, the cost of borrowing drops, thanks to the Federal Reserve lowering interest rates.

This goes back to our history lesson at the start of this chapter. The Fed has consistently used monetary policy to stimulate economic growth, most notably in the last four decades. With each recession since 1981, Federal Reserve chairs since Volcker – the famously cryptic Alan Greenspan (known for his obtuse and hard-to-decipher messages), Ben Bernanke, Janet Yellen and most recently Jerome Powell – have used ever more extreme measures to kickstart the US economy and save it from recession or collapse. Bernanke employed QE – money printing – in 2009, and each successive chair of the Federal Reserve has, at some point during their tenure, employed QE to maintain the stability of the US financial system.

The premise is that if the central bank lowers the cost of borrowing, consumers are all too willing to take advantage of the cheaper money. If we can't become rich through our day jobs, then the central banks can magically allow us to become asset-rich by borrowing up big and fulfilling our dreams of home ownership and building stock portfolios.

Corporations have also been willing to increase their levels of borrowing in response to lower interest rates. Their borrowing has not always been to increase investment in new business activities to grow future earnings, though: since 2008, corporate borrowing has mostly been used to pay out dividends to shareholders and fund share buybacks.

On balance, it is hardly a surprise that as the cost of debt has fallen, there has been a corresponding increase in borrowing and higher levels of debt. However, the rise in the levels of global debt has had a two-pronged impact on the US economy and the world.

First, there has been a negative impact on the ability to grow the US economy as measured by GDP. As interest rates have fallen, levels of debt have risen correspondingly to ever higher amounts. Total US public and private debt has increased almost fourfold – from 167.2% of US GDP in 1980 to an estimated 405% by the end of 2020, according to Hoisington Investment Management Company. As the level of debt has increased, the impact on GDP has decreased. In the September 2020 quarterly Review and Outlook, Hoisington states, 'each additional dollar of debt in 1980 generated a rise in GDP of 60 cents, up from 54 cents in 1940. Since then, this ratio has dropped sharply from 42 cents in 1989 to 27 cents in 2019'. The US economy now requires around $4 of debt to produce $1 of GDP.

The second aspect is what is referred to as the 'financialisation' of the world and how we have moved beyond interest rates being the be-all and end-all to an issue of balance sheets.

### The financialisation of the world

Put simply, financialisation of our world refers to how inter-twined our economies and personal wealth have become with financial assets. Figure 3 overleaf depicts the growth in global financial assets since 1980.

It clearly demonstrates how, because of deregulation of the banking industry, ever-decreasing interest rates and the cheaper cost of borrowing, the world has embraced financial assets such as bonds, stocks (or equities) and gold. According to Statista, in 2019, the finance, insurance, real estate, rental and leasing sector contributed 21% to the US GDP, which was by far the largest sector contribution.

**FIGURE 3: Growth in global financial assets (1980-2020)**

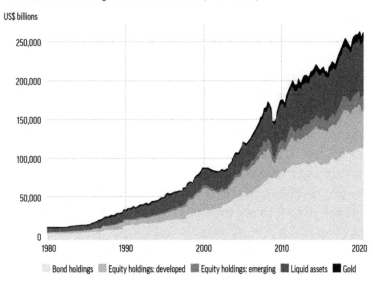

US$ billions

Source: CrossBorder Capital 'Liquidity capital flows and how they affect the investment outlook and conclusions'

In his book *The Great Rupture*, Viktor Shvets reports that the global debt burden was 322% of global GDP – US$250 trillion – at the end of 2019, having risen from US$37 trillion, or 1.5x global GDP, in 1990. The Institute of International Finance has highlighted the impact of the massive QE programme and lower interest rate settings: global debt has surged another US$24 trillion, reaching US$281 trillion by the end of the 2020 or 355% of global GDP.

More worryingly, there are financial instruments valued at anywhere between US$400 trillion to US$800 trillion, which Shvets describes as 'the real level of financialization probably at least four times the global economy and could even be as high as ten times'.

A simple example to explain what Mr Shvets is alluding to is when you take out a mortgage; that loan is then packaged up and repackaged as many as five times to different investors as financial institutions monetise the loan books of lenders. This is not illegal, but it does reflect the depth of gearing in the world's financial systems.

Michael Lewis's bestselling book *The Big Short* (and the consequent movie) about what created the GFC is an excellent reference for further reading if you would like to learn more about how the concept of 'financialisation' has permeated our global financial systems.

The combination of monetary policy and our voracious appetite for debt has turned traditional economic theory on its head. The Federal Reserve once used monetary interest rates to increase economic demand through borrowings and investment, meaning the dog (the economy) wagged the tail (interest rates); now the tail wags the dog.

Through financialisation, the system has become so large and indebted that central banks like the US Federal Reserve must come to the rescue in financial crashes and liquidity contractions, such as in March 2020, with ever greater injections of money. This is what Michael Howell, the Managing Director of CrossBorder Capital, refers to as 'the balance sheet problem'. The global financial system is no longer about how cheap debt is (via interest rates) but about being able to refinance the existing debt. All this debt does not just disappear: it must be repaid or refinanced.

So, what does this mean to you as an investor? Well, the steady downward march in interest rates that caused debt levels to balloon has, in turn, caused the US stock markets – notably the S&P 500 – to experience what has essentially been a 40-year upward trend. Figure 4 depicts how the S&P 500 struggled and fell in the 1970s, but has been in a long-term uptrend since the inflation-busting early 1980s.

**FIGURE 4: S&P 500 1960–2020**

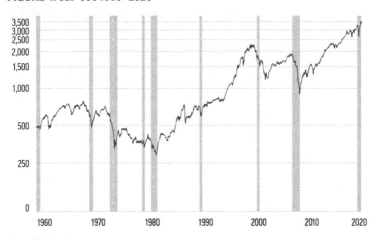

Source: Macrotrends

If we were to overlay Figures 2 and 4, we would see that the drop in interest rates at each grey line (recession) would mark the start of the upward movement in stock prices.

The tremendous long-term returns from US stocks are the result of greater levels of lower-cost debt and bigger balance sheets to support that debt. The US and other world economies are now so dependent on the US stock market's continued ability to generate wealth that the Federal Reserve and other central banks are beholden to supporting the system.

The March 2020 stock market crash is a case in point. The health response to the pandemic – lockdowns – constituted a self-imposed economic slowdown. The spectre of recession or depression then led to the selling of stocks. However, debt in the system meant that once the selling started, some traders and hedge funds could not sell the financial securities they wanted to and instead had to sell other securities to generate cash. The selling created more selling until the system became dysfunctional – there was so much selling and not enough buyers that the financial system stopped working.

It was at that point that the Federal Reserve and other central banks needed to act. Not unlike in the 2008 GFC, there was systemic risk in the financial system. This event catalysed the next round of QE.

To give you some idea of just how much money has entered the system, Figure 5 shows the significant cumulative growth in US liquidity in 2020 compared with 2008–09. The injections of US$3.54 trillion from February to August 2020 dwarf the US$0.46 trillion from October 2008 to January 2009.

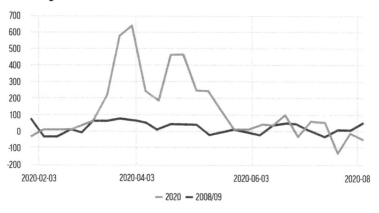

**FIGURE 5:** Cumulative liquidity growth from Oct 2008 to Jan 2009 and from Feb to Aug 2020

Source: CrossBorder Capital

## Where to from here?

As always, 'Where to from here?' is the trillion-dollar question – literally.

Our world has moved into a position where central banks such as the Federal Reserve will need to continue to play an active role in our financial system. This may be an uncomfortable truth for traditionalists, but this is the card we have been dealt.

Balance sheets, lower-for-longer interest rates, large debt levels and the (perceived by some) price bubbles in stocks, property and other assets remain some of the most contentious discussion points for financial experts. For our purposes, it is important that we understand the dynamics of the stock market and what triggers could upset or change them.

Although rises in consumer price inflation have remained elusive since the 2008 GFC (as shown in Figure 1), there is now an expectation from many macro-economic experts that all the money printing and a big-spending US administration will lead to increases in inflation. This will be mirrored by the 10-year US treasury bond rate: if it rises, then the expectation is that inflation and interest rates are going up. From a low of 0.5% in March 2020, the 10-year US treasury has advanced to over 1.774%. Whether it can be maintained above 2%, as the Federal Reserve is targeting, remains to be seen, but inflationary expectations are enough to drive the US bond markets.

How quickly the 10-year US treasury bond rate rises or falls always has a material impact on stock prices. The impact of the 10-year US treasury on stocks and sectors is covered in greater detail in Chapter 8.

Whether experts agree or disagree with the decisions the Federal Reserve and other central banks have made, the point for you is that the debt is here to stay, and confidence in the financial system remains paramount to ensure that the global and US balance sheets remain intact. This means you are likely to see more QE in the future, as well as the Federal Reserve keeping interest rates low as far out as 2024.

The 'lower-for-longer' scenario for interest rates remains good news for US stocks. However, the elusive rise in consumer price inflation poses the biggest concern for stock investors: what will happen if consumer prices start to rise quickly? No one knows, but this looming question will influence how you manage your US stock-picking decisions.

## Chapter summary

► An understanding of macro-economics, known as the 'big picture', provides an invaluable insight into stock market investing.

► The correlation between interest rates and consumer price inflation cannot be ignored, and provides insights into future economic cycles (both contracting and expanding).

► With record levels of debt in both the public and private sectors, money printing (QE) is here to stay according to some experts.

► Confidence in our financial systems is paramount for stock market stability.

# 4

# Valuing the top 20 US giants

So far, we have established that from a big-picture perspective, the outlook for US stocks will at the very least be supported by an accommodative Federal Reserve. In 2020, the chairman, Jerome Powell, and the other members of the Fed underscored their commitment to keeping interest rates low for as long as it takes to increase consumer price inflation to above 2% and to create full employment. The full employment level will vary between countries but is defined as a level of unemployment that is low enough without causing inflation.

The potential for lower-for-longer interest rates relative to historic levels is a positive backdrop for US stocks and the creation of liquidity for those companies that are investing heavily for the future.

The combination of low rates and plentiful liquidity (thanks to a top-up fiscal spending boost to revive the US economy after the pandemic slump) should underscore a robust recovery. And, with the absence of inflation and the 10-year treasury bond rising too quickly, a 'Goldilocks' economy (not too hot nor too cold) offers an optimal stock-investing backdrop.

As you are probably aware (or learning), life in the stock market is not always a fairytale, even in the so-called best of times. No stock price goes up in a straight line forever and volatility is often just a step away, shaking the nerves of even the most experienced experts and the newer investors. For example, a fast upward move in the US 10-year treasury bond rate will spook stock markets with fears of rapidly rising inflation, or better or worse than expected quarterly earnings results.

It's important to remember that not all stocks are ascribed equal valuations and not all stocks make you money. Very few will create long-term wealth. This means we all need to have a sound understanding of what we are buying and why we are buying the stock to weather the storms with any degree of confidence.

Over the next three chapters, I will be looking at the different themes of the US stock markets. As the markets are so large, I'll divide the themes up and explain the differences. Here, in Chapter 4, we'll start by looking at the largest US stocks, including how the category of stock broadly relates to how investors value the stock.

## The three stock categories

At the most basic level, stocks can be divided into the following three categories: defensives, cyclicals and growth.

1. **Defensive stocks** deliver earnings growth through the economic cycles, but may not deliver as much earnings growth as a cyclical stock from the bottom to the top of the cycle. Or they will produce more consistent earnings streams from the top to the bottom of the economic cycle.

2. **Cyclical stocks** deliver higher earnings growth than defensive stocks from the bottom to the top of a cycle and lower growth at the bottom of the cycle.

3.  **Growth stocks** are often the most hotly debated and controversial, which is why I devote two chapters (Chapters 5 and 6) to growth and where to find it.

The problem for most investors is that the noise in the stock markets, and from all the advisers and experts, means there are often multiple and conflicting reasons for what represents value to make you money. It's difficult to understand why an expensive stock (in any category) can keep rising in price, while a cheap stock just keeps falling. This is one of the conundrums of investing and regrettably there is no silver bullet. There are strategies and pathways, however, to finding the answers that suit you and can make you money, which I share with you in this book.

Let's start by examining the differences between some of the largest US companies, or the 'giants' as I will label them. In this book, I have ranked the giants by the amount of sales revenue they generate and by their market capitalisation, which is effectively the valuation given to the stock by investors.

The aim of the revenue versus market capitalisation comparison is to capture, at a point in time, how external influences such as interest rates, economic growth and investor expectations around earnings growth and valuations can shape the performance of a stock.

If you can understand these principles, then you will have a better appreciation of what influences move stocks to make you money. Please bear in mind this is a snapshot and, as markets are dynamic, the numbers change. However, the basic narrative around the giants remains.

## Revenue versus market capitalisation

I could have called this section 'size (revenue) versus valuation' because that's basically the comparison we are exploring.

Fortunately for us, Fortune 500 ranks the largest US companies in terms of 2020 revenues (see Table 1). The companies in *italics* below the top 20 are part of the top 20 largest companies by market capitalisation and not by revenue. I include them here to make comparison easier.

**TABLE 1: US giants ranked by the 2020 sales revenue in US$ millions**

| Rank/name | Revenue ($US m) | Net income ($US m) | Code | Sector (industry) |
|---|---|---|---|---|
| 1. Walmart | 523,964 | 14,881 | WMT | Consumer Staples (Hypermarkets and Super Centers) |
| 2. Amazon | 280,522 | 11,588 | AMZN | Consumer Discretionary (Internet and Direct Marketing) |
| 3. Exxon Mobil | 264,938 | 14,340 | XOM | Energy (Integrated Oil and Gas) |
| 4. Apple | 260,174 | 55,525 | AAPL | Information Technology (Tech hardware, Storage and Peripherals) |
| 5. CVS Health | 256,776 | 6,634 | CVS | Health Care (Health Care Services) |
| 6. Berkshire Hathaway | 254,616 | 81,417 | BRK/B | Financials (Multi-Sector Holdings) |
| 7. UnitedHealth Group | 242,155 | 13,839 | UNH | Health Care (Managed Health Care) |
| 8. McKesson | 214,319 | 34 | MCK | Health Care (Health Care Distributors) |
| 9. AT&T | 181,193 | 13,903 | ATT | Communication Services (Integrated Telecommunications Services) |
| 10. AmerisourceBergen | 179,589 | 855.4 | ABC | Health Care (Health Care Distributors) |
| 11. Alphabet | 161,857 | 34,343 | GOOGL | Communication Services (Interactive Media and Services) |
| 12. Ford Motor Company | 155,900 | 47 | FORD | Consumer Discretionary (Automobile Manufacturers) |
| 13. Cigna | 153,566 | 5,104 | CI | Health Care (Managed Health Care) |
| 14. Costco | 152,703 | 3,659 | COST | Consumer Staples (Hypermarkets and Super Centers) |

| Rank/name | Revenue ($US m) | Net income ($US m) | Code | Sector (industry) |
|---|---|---|---|---|
| 15. Chevron | 146,516 | 2,954 | CVX | Energy (Integrated Oil and Gas) |
| 16. Cardinal Health | 145,534 | 1,363 | CAH | Health Care (Health Care Distributors) |
| 17. JPMorgan Chase | 142,422 | 36,431 | JPM | Financials (Diversified Banks) |
| 18. General Motors | 137,737 | 6,732 | GM | Consumer Discretionary (Automobile Manufacturers) |
| 19. Walgreens Boots Alliance | 136,866 | 3,982 | WBA | Consumer Staples (Drug Retail) |
| 20. Verizon | 131,868 | 19,265 | VZ | Communications Services (Integrated Telecommunication Services) |
| 21. Microsoft | 125,843 | 39,240 | MSFT | Information Technology (Software Systems) |
| 25. Bank of America | 113,589 | 27,430 | BAC | Financials (Diversified Banks) |
| 46. Facebook | 70,697 | 18,485 | FB | Communications (Interactive Media and Services) |
| 49. Walt Disney | 69,570 | 11,054 | DIS | Communications (Movies and Entertainment) |
| 50. Procter & Gamble | 67,684 | 3,897 | PG | Consumer Staples (Personal Products) |
| 124. Tesla | 24,578 | -862 | TSLA | Consumer Discretionary (Automobile Manufacturers) |
| 137. Visa | 22,977 | 12,080 | V | Information Technology (Data Processing & Outsourced Services) |
| 182. PayPal Holdings | 17,772 | 2,459 | PYPL | Information Technology (Data Processing & Outsourced Services) |
| 191. Mastercard | 16,833 | 8,118 | MA | Information Technology (Data Processing & Outsourced Services) |
| 292. Nvidia | 10,918 | 2,796 | NVDA | Information Technology (Semiconductors) |

Source: Fortune 500, CNBC and S&P 500 Stock Market Index

In contrast, Table 2 lists the largest US companies by market capitalisation as at 1 January 2021; the annual return was at the time of writing; and the PER (x) was the future (1 year) earnings. The difference between the two lists tells a story about how investors value stocks.

In Table 2, the companies in *italics* represent the largest companies by revenue that do not appear in the top 20 by market capitalisation.

## TABLE 2: US giants ranked by market capitalisation

| Rank/name | Market cap (US$ b) | Code | Net income (2020 US $ m) | Return on equity (%) | 1 year stock return (%) | PER (x) (future estimates) |
|---|---|---|---|---|---|---|
| 1. Apple | 2255 | AAPL | 57,411 | 82.09 | +75.54 | 32.92 |
| 2. Microsoft | 1681 | MSFT | 44,281 | 42.70 | +38.69 | 32.26 |
| 3. Amazon | 1634 | AMZN | 21,331 | 27.44 | +69.96 | 66 |
| 4. Alphabet | 1185 | GOOG GOOGL | 40,269 | 19.00 | +27.01 | 30.68 |
| 5. Facebook | 778 | FB | 29,146 | 25.42 | +28.88 | 26.91 |
| 6. Tesla | 668 | TSLA | 721 | 4.78 | +723.65 | 325 |
| 7. Berkshire Hathaway | 543 | BRK.B | 42,521 | 9.80 | +1.0 | 24.58 |
| 8. Visa | 511 | V | 10,886 | 32.47 | +15.57 | 39.88 |
| 9. Johnson & Johnson | 414 | JNJ | 14,714 | 23.49 | +11.45 | 19.61 |
| 10. Walmart | 407 | WMT | 13,510 | 17.37 | +26.38 | 26.08 |
| 11. JPMorgan Chase | 387 | JPM | 29,131 | 11.33 | -5.63 | 16.5 |
| 12. Mastercard | 355 | MA | 6,411 | 104.38 | +17.61 | 55.53 |
| 13. Procter & Gamble | 343 | PG | 13,027 | 29.55 | +15.21 | 24.72 |
| 14. UnitedHealth Group | 332 | UNH | 15,403 | 25.02 | +22.65 | 20.86 |
| 15. Walt Disney | 328 | DIS | -2,864 | -5.67 | +21.28 | 98.27 |
| 16. Nvidia | 323 | NVDA | 4332 | 29.78 | +122.57 | 53.91 |

| Rank/name | Market cap (US$ b) | Code | Net income (2020 US $ m) | Return on equity (%) | 1 year stock return (%) | PER (x) (future estimates) |
|---|---|---|---|---|---|---|
| 17. Home Depot | 285 | HD | 12,866 | 14,601.73 | +23.44 | 22.22 |
| 18. PayPal | 274 | PYPL | 4,202 | 22.77 | +113.24 | 61.26 |
| 19. Bank of America | 262 | BAC | 17,894 | 6.73 | -11.64 | 17.14 |
| 20. Verizon | 243 | VZ | 17,801 | 27.55 | +1.71 | 12.19 |
| AT&T | 209 | T | -5,176 | -3.10 | -19.48 | 9.51 |
| Exxon Mobil | 175 | XOM | -22,440 | -12.88 | -36.28 | 19.11 |
| Costco | 168.39 | COST | 4002 | 26.93 | +34.81 | 37.27 |
| Chevron | 163 | CVX | -5543 | -4.02 | -26.05 | 20.87 |
| CVS | 92.23 | CVS | 7,179 | 10.79 | -1.58 | 9.57 |
| Cigna | 74.32 | CI | 8,458 | 17.68 | +1.27 | 11 |
| General Motors | 57.98 | GM | 6427 | 14.39 | +12.94 | 8.65 |
| Walgreen Boots Alliance | 35.77 | WBA | 456 | -3.59 | -26.79 | 8.74 |
| McKesson | 28.2 | MCK | 900 | -147.06 | | 11.20 |
| Ford Motor Company | 27.62 | FORD | -1,279 | -4.00 | -14.29 | 40 |
| AmerisourceBergen | 19.7 | ABC | -3,408 | -285.42 | +16.89 | 11.49 |
| Cardinal Health | 15.53 | CAH | -3.696 | 93.06 | +11.45 | 9.04 |

Source: Bloomberg and CNBC

The rest of the chapter discusses the key findings revealed in these tables. Our reference point is the top 20 giants by market capitalisation as this offers a better idea of how investors value stocks rather than just the size of the company as judged by revenue.

## Growth drove stock prices in 2020

Only four stocks occupy the rarefied valuations of the trillion-dollar market cap club. They are, of course, the 'global' technology behemoths that are controversial both for their size and for the power they wield. Apple, Microsoft, Amazon and Alphabet (the parent of Google) have surprised cynics and naysayers for as long as I can remember. All have disrupted or changed the industries they operate in and are global players in some of the highest growth sectors in the world: mobile telephony, computer hardware, software, the cloud, ecommerce, digitalisation, online advertising, internet search engines and data collection. All were beneficiaries of lower interest rates and the lockdown economies of the 2020 stay-at-home period.

Apple, Amazon, Nvidia and PayPal were standout growth giants for 2020 with the highest stock price appreciations (excluding Tesla). These companies were fortunate enough to have services and products suited to the demand generated from the global pandemic and the stay-at-home economy.

In these four examples, strong earnings and high profitability (in spite of the deep recessions) were rewarded with great stock price returns and, therefore, high market cap valuations.

Apple remains a beneficiary of the newly released 5G technology via its phone and related hardware and software products. Apple's valuation is supported by the move to the more sustainable and recurring revenue streams produced by its App Store products and services, which continue to show strong growth. Between Christmas Eve and New Year's Eve, 2020, App Store sales rose 27% year-on-year (yoy) compared to 19% yoy growth in 2019. Apple continues to generate earnings growth through the App Store and, longer term, an Apple autonomous electric vehicle is mooted to be released by 2024.

Amazon's ability to develop and grow its ecommerce dominance (for example through Amazon Prime), as well as the cloud services (through Amazon Web Services (AWS)), has not abated. As much as we all think ecommerce cannot develop any further, we need to remember that online sales still only made up 19.3% of total retail sales in the US as at the third quarter of 2020. The pandemic accelerated the transfer of retail shopping from traditional bricks and mortar (shopping malls and centres) to online by as much as 37% yoy. In the USA, every $1 out of $5 is now spent online. In contrast, one of the oldest and best-known retailers in the USA, Macy's, is shuttering 125 stores by 2023, retaining only those stores operating in what are called 'A' class malls. Is it any wonder so many experts argue there remains considerable scope for increased growth in online sales?

Walmart, the largest employer and revenue generator in the US, is not taking the ecommerce and online sales disruption lightly. Their ecommerce sales grew 79% yoy in the third quarter of 2020.

As well as being a beneficiary of the stay-at-home economy in 2020, the company remains innovative and is adapting to technological change by improving its online offering and expanding into payment services. This has resulted in its number-ten ranking in the market cap valuations.

Microsoft and Alphabet (Google's parent) also score high market cap valuations, even though their revenue doesn't rank as highly as some of the more traditional companies. Both these technology companies are extremely profitable and generated net income in the high to mid-$30 billions, respectively. Microsoft just keeps on growing through the expansion of its existing businesses and acquisitions, as well as the growth in the cloud computing business, Azure.

Google is outstanding for the fact that it managed to perform well in lockdowns and is now a major beneficiary (as is Facebook) of the economic reopening and reflation trade through the increased advertising spend, as more people and companies move back to more normal behaviour.

This leads me to highlight the next point: although these behemoths do not generate the highest revenues in the US, they are all well above the net income generators (meaning they are highly profitable as per the return on equity ratio). They are also global giants, benefiting from massive tailwinds from secular megatrend growth (more about this in Chapters 5 and 6).

These giants are perceived as benefiting from the ultra-low interest rate environment too.

Conversely the cheaper, value stocks (often with highly cyclical earnings), which performed poorly in 2020 due to the deep recession, stand to perform better when the US economy recovers – as reflected by a rising US 10-year treasury bond yield.

One of the most challenging aspects for investors is to understand the dynamics of how interest rates and, predominantly, the US 10-year treasury bond affect stock prices. (Chapters 8 and 9 take a more in-depth look into why changing interest rates can affect stock valuations.)

If growth was the 2020 winning formula, then the value/cyclical stocks seem set to take up the baton in 2021 with the US economic recovery.

Let's move through the list of giants and establish some more of the trends that emerged in 2020 to obtain a better understanding of how the experts look at the markets.

### Old versus new energy

Tables 1 and 2 presented earlier in the chapter showed a vexing stock investment conundrum. Why does a company as large as Exxon Mobil (in revenue terms) have such a low (relatively speaking) market cap, and could that change? Cyclical, energy, commodity-based companies like Exxon are basically beholden to the input price of the products they produce, in this case oil and gas. Take just one look at the historical price chart of crude oil in Figure 6 and you will see how volatile the price can be.

**FIGURE 6: Crude oil price (1990–2020)**

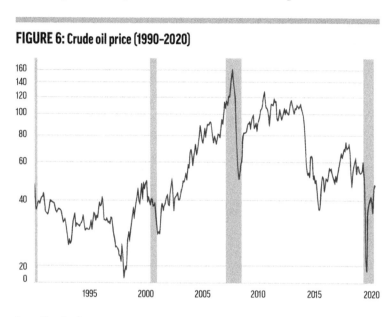

Source: Macrotrends

The crude oil market is considerably more complex than just supply and demand. The OPEC cartel works to manage oil price stability by expanding and contracting supply. This means a company will be profitable according to the price it receives for the oil, the cost of production, whether it is increasing or cutting back on exploration and new reserves and the outlook for the energy-commodity.

You can see clearly from Figure 6 how the during the 2007–2009 GFC recession, oil and gas prices collapsed. This happened again during the enforced lockdowns and deep recession of the 2020 pandemic. (The grey vertical bars depict recessions.)

Let's look now at the share price of Exxon Mobil over the same period (see Figure 7).

**FIGURE 7:** Exxon Mobil share price (1990–2020)

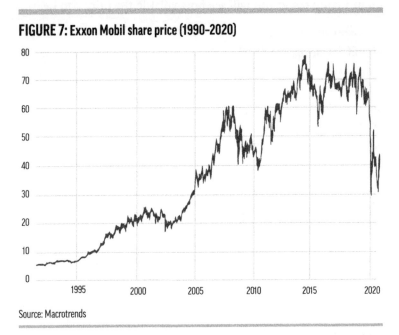

Source: Macrotrends

The correlation between the crude oil price and the performance of the stock price is immediately evident.

It's hardly surprising that in the deepest recession (depression) since the 1930s, nearly 100 years ago, the crude oil price collapse in 2020 (as demand crashed during the lockdowns) meant oil and gas companies not only struggled to make profits but also that their stock prices fell. For Exxon, the story goes deeper. Lower oil prices led to lower cash flow and losses, as well as higher debt needed to fund an overzealous dividend payment to stockholders.

Exxon plans to cut its capital expenditure and investment by US$10 billion p.a. and focus on its value assets. The company has been forced to write down the value of its assets by US$20 billion in 2020, as it was such a punishing year. In essence, the year was an *annus horribilis* for Exxon and the proof was in the performance or lack thereof of the stock price (down 36% in 2020) and their ranking of 175 in terms of market capitalisation. Note that the return on equity was also very poor.

In stark contrast, Exxon's nemesis, the clean energy and electric vehicle manufacturer Tesla, was one of the stock market's best performers in 2020, up over 700% for those lucky stockholders.

So, what gives? Why can a relatively new (I use that term loosely, as 20 years is a lot younger than over 100 years) company that only produced just shy of 500,000 vehicles be ascribed the number 6 slot on the top 20 giants market cap rating?

The short answer is that more investors at this point in time think the change-maker Tesla will be a winner as the global economies transition away from fossil fuels. Tesla may not be largest electric vehicle manufacturer in a decade, but the market believes it has *at this point in time* the greatest chance of achieving that goal of producing 20 million EVs across ten giga factories on major continents. (To provide some context, that target is double the current production of either Toyota or Volkswagen, in a marketplace of around one billion vehicles.)

As well as full vertical integration of the world's lowest-cost electric vehicle production and becoming the best in the market for production, brand and product, Tesla is operating in many other growth sectors, including batteries, solar panels and autonomous and full self-driving-vehicle software-as-a-service (SaaS), with the potential extension of the SaaS capacity to a robotaxi fleet.

The Tesla growth plan may seem like a pipedream and its valuation beyond excessive, but the more Tesla can live up to and exceed these often-touted outrageous goals and expectations, the more the stock will be rewarded with a high valuation.

Equally, the more the legacy automotive manufacturers (think General Motors, Ford and Volkswagen) and multiple relative newcomers like Tesla succeed with electric and clean-energy vehicles, the greater the probability that the oil price will become volatile, and producers will need to reduce production costs to remain competitive as the total value and production of oil shrinks. Demand for oil will not disappear overnight – the world is currently far too dependent on it to change that paradigm so quickly – but the shift to non-gasoline alternatives will fundamentally reshape the oil production market.

Exxon's strategic move to the higher value, better quality projects is proof that this behemoth, started by John D. Rockefeller in the 1880s, sees the landscape changing.

The long-term story, however, contrasts with how some investors will treat Exxon in the case of an economic upturn, as is forecast for 2021 and beyond. The bottom line is buyers will seek out a company like Exxon to benefit from a rise in the oil price, due to cyclical factors.

Tesla's appeal to investors will depend on a multitude of factors, not least of which is whether the company is able to produce tangible results and kick more of its ambitious goals.

## Payment giants benefit from the pandemic

Although not the largest revenue generators, global payment giants Visa, Mastercard and PayPal were fortunate enough to benefit from the stay-at-home/work-at-home economy and the trend in non-cash and contactless payment systems in 2020. The growth in these sectors can be correlated to the boom in digital ecommerce. Arguably, all these trends were boosted by the pandemic and the need to avoid the spread of the coronavirus.

Not only is the status of cash as king being challenged by monetary policy (money printing by the Fed has the potential to undermine the status of the US dollar), but also the pandemic has all but tolled the death knell for the use of cash in retail. (Payment systems and the evolution of new lending and ecommerce transactions are important themes that I discuss in more detail in Chapter 6.)

Although the valuations of the payment giants are not cheap, any uptick in economic activity will benefit their earnings. However, disruption is never far away and buy-now-pay-later companies such as Afterpay, Affirm and Klarna, to name just three, are challenging the traditional payments system of credit cards.

## Dreaming and streaming

I am regrettably old enough to remember watching Disney's Sunday evening programme on free-to-air television and delighting in each new, wonderful tale as espoused by the theme song, 'When you wish upon a star'.

The classic entertainment firm Disney (Walt Disney Company) has achieved the remarkable feat of coming in at number 15 in the giants' market cap rankings, even though 2020 was one of the most challenging trading years on record. The Disney theme parks and cruise liners were shuttered and staff furloughed during the pandemic, but the strength of the Disney name and its library of remarkable content lived on, in spite of cinema and theatre closures, because of the launch of its online streaming channel Disney+.

Online content and streaming services may have existed pre-pandemic, but their growth accelerated considerably through 2020. Disney has the advantage of not only having a catalogue of world-beating content, but also of having the potential to recover further when US and global economies reopen as vaccines roll out.

In essence, Disney is a survivor because of its willingness to adapt to challenging economic circumstances; and, of course, it possesses the assets and potential to generate high revenues when life returns to normal. Although its stock is not cheap, Disney stands to benefit from secular growth in streaming services as well as cyclical growth with the reopening of trade.

## Health care and pharma face challenges

The health care space has some of the largest giants, both in terms of revenue and market cap, but there is a distinct line between the haves and the have-nots in this sector. In part, the challenges to companies in this sector are driven by disruption, regulatory changes and the increasing costs of health care.

UnitedHealth Group and Johnson & Johnson fall into the 'haves', both sitting in the top 20 by market cap rankings. UnitedHealth is America's largest health insurer and has been able to continue to deliver good earnings growth, as has Johnson & Johnson, which is also one of the vaccine-providers.

Drug manufacturers AmerisourceBergen and Cardinal are both struggling 'have-nots' embroiled in major lawsuits over their involvement in the US opioid crisis, and one of the world's largest drugstore (chemist) operators Walgreen Boots Alliance faces disruption from Amazon and Walmart. Integrated pharmaceutical company CVS also operates drugstores and may benefit from the rollout of the vaccines, although I understand the instore customer experience is perceived by some as underwhelming.

Generally speaking, health care and pharmaceutical stocks are defensive earnings companies. They do well whether economic activity is good or poor, as our aging populations globally underpin long-term demand for their products and services.

However, like many industries, the high margins the industry enjoys make it ripe for disruption and increased competition. Although a three-way venture into health care from Amazon, Berkshire Hathaway and JPMorgan has been cancelled, there remains a sustained push from other giants (and smaller online digital players) to grab a piece of the health care pie.

The increased competition will have an ongoing impact on margins for the incumbents and, like the technology giants, regulatory changes from the left wing of the Democratic Party may impact on the sector.

As a rule of thumb, some of the more expensive health care stocks may have their stock prices challenged if there are signs of rising interest rates, while others may continue to benefit from the pandemic. The cheaper value stocks will likely attract bottom-fishing value buyers.

## Banks

JPMorgan Chase and Bank of America are banking giants. Although they're well capitalised and resilient, stock prices of all banks around the globe fell sharply in 2020 when the economic recessions hit. Banks are impacted three-fold by:

1. A slowdown in economic activity and therefore lending
2. An increase in provisions for bad debts

3. A squeeze on their margins as the long end of the interest rate curve fell sharply as the Fed dropped interest rates and used QE to control interest rates further.

It is testament to the size and quality of JPMorgan that the bank remained in the top 20 giants in spite of 2020 being such a tough year. There is an expectation of improved economic activity as the 10-year treasury rises on the back of the vaccine rollout and, to some degree, the Democrat election win brings anticipation of a big-spending government. Higher government spending will most likely increase interest costs for the country: hence the rise in the 10-year treasury.

Banks, including these two giants, are very much a part of the reflation theme – with the reopening of the economy as the vaccines roll out.

Longer term disruption and potentially lower-for-longer interest rates will challenge the banks' business models. Like many an industry suffering the effects of digitalisation and disruption, the banks will have to move with the change and adapt.

## Telecommunication challenges

AT&T and Verizon remain the telco giants, and both offer a good dividend yield. However, even with the expected growth in 5G rollouts and resulting increased earnings, both these companies remain cheaply valued and their business models are challenged.

Telco companies around the developed world have all suffered from significant cost pressures (rolling out and maintaining networks and bidding for new spectrums like 5G do not come cheap). They also face competition from smaller operators as well as from mobile telephony and streaming services.

For example, both AT&T and Verizon need to invest around US$15 to US$20 billion per year and another US$8 to US$10 billion in maintaining the networks. Often, the full cost benefit is not passed down to the hardware suppliers like Verizon and AT&T from consumers like you and me. The consistent decline in telephony service prices has been the cause of ongoing struggle for these giants. The internet is much cheaper, the cost of phone calls is much cheaper and how many of you still have a landline?

The disruption of the telecommunications sector will remain a constant and earnings for both these giants have been low since the GFC. Verizon, on balance, has fared better, delivering a high share price performance and some earnings growth.

## (Smaller) giants that didn't make the cut

Before we recap on this chapter, it is worth highlighting that the size and the depth of the US stock markets and, in this case, the S&P 500, are such that global household names such as Coca-Cola, Nike, Netflix, Pfizer, Merck, Salesforce and McDonald's don't make the top 20.

Like the giants discussed, some of these smaller giants will be dealing with challenges of disruption and change.

McDonald's is adapting to online food-delivery services, meatless hamburgers and improved health quality of its fast-food offering. Netflix continues to grow and challenge the entertainment industry. Although debates swirl around the company, with experts questioning its valuation and the scope to grow its subscriber base, I would challenge any of you who have enjoyed the trend in streaming entertainment via Amazon Prime, Apple, Disney or even Stan down-under (in Australia) to believe that this service is going anywhere soon.

Salesforce, one of the fastest growing (through acquisitions) software-as-a-service (SaaS) companies, made its debut in 2020 on the Dow Jones index. Although not as richly valued as some other SaaS companies, the general expectation is that growth companies like Salesforce may not perform as well in 2021 if the reflation trade (higher economic activity and interest rates) continues, but longer term prospects remain good.

## Chapter summary

- When it comes to the stock markets, companies classified as growth – such as the technology giants – will benefit from lower interest rates (or the expectation thereof).

- Investors always value growth in earnings. Cyclical and value companies perform better when there is an expected reflation of economic growth, because these companies have operating leverage to the economic cycle.

- Long-term secular trends and technological disruption will continue to cut across many companies and industries. Tapping into those themes can boost earnings and revenue growth.

- Knowing the company you are investing in and the reason you are investing remains important as the tussle between value and growth themes and secular versus cyclical continues in 2021 and beyond.

# Secular megatrends:
# part one - an overview

Leaving behind macro-economics and the top 20 giants, we're now getting to the part of the book where we start to look at more US stocks. To understand the companies that have the potential to make millions over the next decade, we have to explore secular megatrends.

The topic of secular megatrends is so broad that I have split it into two chapters. This chapter offers you an overview of secular investing and how to value growth stocks in the secular mega-trend markets. Then, Chapter 6 explores some specific growth sectors and looks at individual stocks.

If you are not familiar with the term 'secular megatrends', then put simply: secular growth is a fundamental change in a sector that creates strong long-term demand for a new product or service that well exceeds the traditional cyclical upturns in economic activity. Let's leave it to Macquarie Bank's global equities strategist and big thinker Viktor Shvets to define 'megatrends':

> 'Robotics, cloud computing, AI and 3D printing are
> revolutionizing energy, manufacturing and consumption.

Beyond atoms lies the singularity (the inability to differentiate between human and non-human contribution).'

(This quote is from his book *The Great Rupture*.) Viktor Shvets belongs to a group of experts who assert that we are on the cusp of the greatest yet technological innovation and disruption with the rollout of the 21st century's secular megatrends over the next two decades and beyond.

I want you all to envisage autonomous robotaxis, smart appliances, smart clean-energy systems and digital Bitcoin wallets. All these innovations include or are part of the acceleration of DANCE, an anacronym which stands for the growth business sectors of data, algorithms, networks, cloud computing and improved digital hardware. The lines between traditional hardware and software businesses are becoming increasingly blurred as smart hardware embraces cloud-operated software as a service (SaaS). As technology analyst Laura Martin stated:

> 'AAPL (Apple) should be valued as an ecosystem company owing to its seamless integration of hardware, software and content, we believe.'

Yes, I can hear the guffaws of doubters and naysayers, but I wager that you will make more money by investing in the winning companies – or the 'best in breed/sector/class' of change-makers – in the third decade of 21st-century megatrends than buying mature businesses in cyclical sectors.

## The winning stocks: few and far between

We all have intuition and hunches when it comes to investing, but did you know that most stocks will not give you the returns you are aiming for?

Professor Hendrik Bessembinder's study 'Do stocks outperform Treasury bills?' is seminal for many reasons. Arguably, the most valuable takeaway is just how few stocks in the US stock markets have produced positive results for investors over time when compared to the relatively risk-free option of buying US bonds (treasuries).

The study showed how short the life cycle is for most listed companies (seven years on average), and that out of the universe of 26,000 stocks analysed between 1926 and 2015, less than 4% of the top 1000 stocks resulted in the US$32 trillion of wealth creation above bonds over that period.

Investing in stocks is not only about wealth creation: it is a means to grow our savings and protect against the erosion in the value of savings through inflation. Therefore, we are seeking a return that is higher than what the experts call the 'risk-free rate', usually cited as the US 10-year treasury bond.

The fact that so few stocks are real winners is a stark reminder that not all stocks are created equal, and picking the winners is as important as avoiding the losers.

In Chapter 4, you learnt about the US giants and how the stock market views valuations and investing in cyclical versus growth companies. The analysis revealed how many of the so-called 'value/cyclical' stocks and old-economy stocks have been out of favour, and the reasons for this were explained.

Not all cyclical stocks are created equal: commodity, metal and minerals and energy stocks can benefit from super-cycles of demand – think iron ore prices in 2008 and 2020. The stock price appreciation for such stocks can equal, if not exceed, that of growth stocks, but a rising demand and higher end-price products inevitably lead to more supply. Depending upon the speed and cost of the new production and sources of supplies, the price for metals, minerals and energy sources can fall.

In general, stocks that generate earnings from the input price of whatever they produce are subject to the vagaries of demand and supply. Other cyclical value stocks such as property, banking and credit providers can experience a stock-price pop for a while and may seemingly offer value. However, disruption and disintermediation (the streamlining of services to reduce costs and the middleman – e.g. direct lending and banking between customers without a bank branch) can threaten future earnings prospects.

The same uncertainties could possibly apply to the major global giants of FAANMG (Facebook, Apple, Amazon, Netflix, Microsoft and Google) discussed in Chapter 4. The question we all need to ask ourselves is will the four trillion-dollar giants still hold their positions as the largest US stocks in 10 years' time? My hunch is that one or two of them might, but history has shown that companies are most profitable before they die. According to Viktor Shvets, their ascendancy has peaked when they start 'self-liquidating' with share buybacks, meaning they have so much extra cash they start buying back their stock to improve the earnings per stock.

When it comes to predicting the future, the evolution and adoption of the secular megatrends mentioned at the start of this chapter may take longer than expected, and some may fail completely. Disruptive innovation comes with risks and uncertainties. The winners will be tremendous wealth-creators but, as markets evolve, many losers will fall by the wayside. Learning how to pick the winning companies that have the ability to adapt, grow and succeed in spite of risks such as regulatory hurdles, politics, legal challenges and competition is your pathway to successful investing.

In Chapter 8, you will discover the 'secret sauce' of what characteristics will define a winning company and how you can structure a winning US stock portfolio, but for now let's look at some winning growth stocks.

## Secular growth trends

Ecommerce is a great example of a secular growth trend. Online retail sales in the US grew from around 0.5% of total retail sales in 1999 to around 20% by the end of 2020.

Secular trends can be impacted by changes in economic activity of a more cyclical nature, but are generally perceived to be more resilient than traditional cyclical business models and sectors, as demand can be sustained or grow during economic downturns (this is due to disruption or switching when consumers change from the older business to the newer one). In the case of the pandemic, a mix of enforced lockdowns and limits on discretionary expenditure for travel, tourism and the like substantially increased demand for online services and goods, taking demand away from traditional bricks and mortar (physical shops).

According to James L. Callinan from Osterweis Capital Management, there are three drivers of secular growth:

1.  **Foundational technology:** This is the most profound innovation and change-maker. There are many examples over history in which technology not only allows for the evolution of a new marketplace, but also many businesses and other technologies leverage or build from the innovative development. Examples include electricity from combustion engines and, more recently, ecommerce from the internet.

2.  **Replacement product, existing market:** This is relatively self-explanatory: technology allows for the development of a replacement product or service that challenges the incumbent legacy producers. Companies use these products and services to grow their sales and market share – and erode the market share of existing players. They do this by offering cheaper, more efficient or better services or goods; or those that meet changing market dynamics. I don't want

to sound like a broken record, but the electric vehicle is a current example. In bygone days, it was the dishwasher or washing machine.

3. **New product, new market:** Osterweis cites Google as a great example of a new service (providing search and advertising engines) that was founded and built upon what was a new communications and information transfer network, the internet. Google's market share has grown to 92% of all internet searches, having wiped out the competition since the early days of the late 1990s. Arguably, with such market dominance, a company like Google is not only attracting possible regulatory intervention, but its growth has moved from secular to cyclical (as it benefits from an uptick in advertising spend). When companies achieve market dominance, the ability to further grow revenue and earnings becomes more dependent on economic cycles and the ability to innovate and adapt.

This leads to what we are looking for in secular growth companies, the 'S' curve, as you can see in Figure 8.

**FIGURE 8: The S Curve**

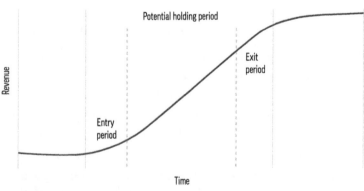

The S curve shows sales revenue from a new business model. Initially, it takes time for the product or service to develop and sales to grow, but once the adaptation, demand and popularity increase, sales have the potential to grow very strongly (see the mid-section of the curve in Figure 8). If the company fails to change and adapt through reinvesting, then it is likely the sales of the once innovator or change-maker will slow down, as shown by the flattening of the curve.

The valuations given to companies on the S curve will change over the course of the curve as well. For example, in bull markets such as we saw in 2020, there was a lot of liquidity generated by the Fed and most secular stocks rose, and often rose steeply, even if the business was at the entry point. This meant investors were giving the company the benefit of the doubt in terms of its future growth potential, referred to as a 'long earnings tail', when earnings come well in the future. If the market thinks a stock will grow its revenue and earnings at a high compound average growth rate (CAGR), the total addressable market (TAM) is huge. In bull markets, with low interest rates, these stocks will be given crazy-high valuations, equal to and in excess of 50x a price-to-sales ratio. Investors may well look back at these valuations as excessive 'bubble'-like multiples in a low interest rate world.

Many of the growth S curve start-ups have no reported earnings and their valuations are derived from the price-to-sales (revenue) multiple. (Valuation metrics will be explained in more detail later in this chapter and in Chapters 6, 8 and 9.)

However, if there are any indications of a slowdown in revenue growth (either reported or indicated via the company's outlook), the stock price is normally sold down heavily. This means a stock's valuation will either contract or expand depending on whether the company can successfully execute the next phase of high revenue growth to penetrate the large TAM.

A good example is the software company Zoom Media, which offers online video conferencing. Zoom was far from the first to offer video streaming and webinars, but the ease of use and the improved service that it offers, compared with Skype and Microsoft Teams for example, made Zoom a top performer in the lockdown economies of the pandemic. Its stock price rose from US$70 in late February 2020 to a high of US$568 in October 2020 before successful vaccine treatments started being announced. Zoom's stock price then retraced to around $350.

The Zoom example shows how quickly the S curve effect can take hold. In 2020, the company more than tripled its revenue; however, the rollout of the vaccine has given the market cause to reconsider its growth prospects in the future. Will Zoom be able to continue to grow revenue at the 2020 rate with a perceived return to business-as-usual with reopenings? Can Zoom continue to adapt to the changing macro-environment? Even expert analysts do not know the answers to these questions with certainty. However, those investors who understand the company well will be able to make a calculated estimate of Zoom's future growth potential, including its ability to successfully roll out new services such as Zoom phone.

## Fair reasonable price

The markets can often push stock prices well ahead of what is considered a fair or reasonable price, particularly when optimism about secular growth is fuelled by cheap money. Many would argue that Tesla is one such stock. Scott Galloway, Professor of Marketing at NYU Stern, calls them 'story stocks'.

You should never underestimate the appeal of a great story and how our brain can legitimise a story to pay any price for a stock. This is when we need to keep the emotional exuberance or greed in check.

Philip A. Fisher, author of the phenomenally successful *Common Stocks and Uncommon Profits*, believes that many stock enthusiasts 'know the price of everything and the value of nothing'.

All investors should aim to seek out stocks that can offer 'growth at a reasonable price' or 'GARP' in finance jargon. Ideally, you want to pick through the companies or sectors that will offer the mega-growth of the S curve at a reasonable price. If you pay too much upfront for future earnings, which can happen in bull markets, you may be disappointed when either the macroeconomic conditions change (e.g. the Fed stops printing money or inflation/interest rates go up) or the stock doesn't live up to the secular growth expectations and earnings disappoint.

Always remember, even the best wealth-creators in secular markets cannot grow earnings in a straight line. However, you do want to own those stocks that are resilient to the challenges of competition, innovation and disruption and can continue to develop and grow.

## Spotting the mega-secular growth sectors and the stocks

When you are confronted with the onerous challenge of trying to determine what sectors and what stocks to buy in the US (or anywhere else for that matter), it is good to remind yourself of the traditional concept of what are referred to as the 'big' and the 'small' pictures or the 'top-down' and 'bottom-up' approaches.

I like the following quote from Louis A. Stevens (from Stevens Investments LLC), as the statement captures the concept in a way that is relevant to the world of disruptive innovation and technology in which we are living:

'I like to think of my team and myself as scientists with two primary tools in hand: a microscope for businesses and a telescope for mankind's future. Our microscope allows us to avoid overpaying and our telescope allows us to glimpse into the future of business to ensure we're buying the next Apples (NASDAQ: AAPL), Amazons (NASDAQ: AMZN), and Facebooks (NASDAQ: FB).'

You are not expected to be the scientist doing all the number-crunching and hard analytics. All you need to do is keep your eyes wide open and be receptive to new ideas, with both your metaphoric telescope and your microscope. The experts will fill in the gaps.

To help you on your way, Chapter 6 will outline all the major galaxies or mega-secular growth sectors your microscope needs to target, either through direct stock investing, or investing through ETFs or managed funds in the following chapters.

But, before we move onto the sectors and stocks, I want to work through some of the ways in which growth stocks are valued.

## Valuing growth companies

Value investors assess stock valuations using fundamental analysis, such as price-to-earnings ratios, the price discount-to-net-asset value or a dividend discount model (discounting the future income stream from a stock to provide a current valuation). They would, for the greater part, consider the analysis used to value technology companies and secular growth stocks as 'voodoo valuations' or speculative madness.

Why is this?

Growth stocks, such as software companies (SaaS) generally report high revenue growth and no earnings, as the company will be reinvesting much of the cash flow generated into the future growth of the business. Growth businesses in the 21st century are often referred to as 'weightless' technology companies, meaning they operate and invest in software, data analytics and machine learning – not physical assets such as bricks and mortar, plant and equipment. Growth companies typically, but not always, are more prevalent in the 'weightless' sectors or have a stronger technological slant to their business model. Growth companies are growth because they are usually at the start of the S curve.

More mature and normally cyclical businesses have pre-existing (fully depreciated) plant and equipment (hard assets) and they aim to grow revenue and earnings through an uptick in economic demand and/or product improvements, introducing new products, gaining market share, expanding into new markets and/or cost cutting, or increasing margins via some other avenue such as reducing the number of employees and reducing advertising spend.

Growth stocks, conversely, are still witnessing strong demand and the constraints are not always related to demand issues but issues on the supply side.

You could be forgiven if you thought growth investing was a new investing style, given the media coverage devoted to the technology giants and the talk about another dotcom-like bubble. However, there have been three periods in history when growth stocks were dominant, and these times are often cited by value investors as reasons *not* to buy growth stocks. Each period was marked by varying degrees of euphoric investor behaviour and all were followed by stock market crashes. In some cases, prolonged periods followed when the market for listed stocks went completely out of favour.

The three examples are:

1. The 1920s, until the 1929 crash that preceded the Great Depression.

2. The 1960s – when a group of popular stocks, including Xerox, AVON, Coca-Cola, Eastman Kodak, Gillette, Polaroid and

Xerox were referred to as the 'Nifty 50'; the last golden period for equities pre the 1973–74 stock market crash.

3. The 2000–01 dotcom (tech and telecom) bubble.

In all three cases, the valuations for popular stocks, usually perceived as the 'growth' stocks of the day, were pushed to what some experts felt was characteristic of greed-fuelled investor euphoria. In the dotcom bubble, investors were overly optimistic about the potential long growth runways from the 'internet' technology,s when, in reality, it took another 15 years for the technology to properly evolve. Amazon is a case in point.

I chanced upon an excellent quote from legendary investor Charlie Munger of Berkshire Hathaway in May 2020, who described the Nifty 50 'as absolute dementia'. Since most of us weren't investing in the 1960s, Mr Munger, who has lived through multiple stock market cycles from 1962, was able to share his wisdom. He was incredulous that a home sewing company, Simplicity Patterns, could have traded at 50x forward earnings. Ultimately, companies like Simplicity were given outrageous valuations and their business models were up-ended by the shift from homemakers and housewives sewing their own clothes to them buying cheap fast fashion.

Other stocks in the Nifty 50 are also a shadow of their former selves. They include AVON, Eastman Kodak, Polaroid and Xerox. Even the original technology behemoths – IBM, Dell and Intel – are experiencing severe competitive pressures, which are eroding sales from disruption, and they are unable to keep pace with innovation.

These examples show what is wrong with investing in growth stocks. But, as is so often the case in financial circles, generalisations around growth need to be clarified and placed into some context.

Not all companies are created equal and the winners can see through the bad times. So be careful not to lump everything into one basket or what some experts call a 'factor' (e.g. growth or value). Walmart has been a winning stock since the era of the Nifty 50 and continues to adapt and grow; even if its valuation no longer suggests it is a growth stock, it has nevertheless given investors solid, long-term returns.

Let's round off this discussion by remembering that not all stocks were frauds or wannabes in the dotcom bubble of 2000–01. Arguably, if you had bought Amazon around the lows of September 2001 for US$8, you'd now be holding the stock at US$3300. If you had invested US$5000 in Amazon in late September 2001, your holding would be worth over US$2 million.

As is always the case with investing in stocks, the devil is in the detail. Paying too much for a stock can happen whether it is a value cyclical company or a growth stock. But, even if you pay too much for a company that continues to generate growth, you will make money over the longer term.

## Stock price performance and revenue growth

Before you learn more about growth stocks, I want to pause to consider how stock price performance has been correlated to revenue growth. Some commentators might consider the following charts simplistic; however, the stock market is often very simplistic. The charts show how money-making potential varies profoundly between those companies that are able to generate revenue growth and those companies that stumble.

Figure 9 depicts four US stocks – Amazon and Apple (growth stocks) and IBM and Intel (value, cyclical stocks, more mature businesses) and their revenue growth in US dollars.

**FIGURE 9:** Revenue growth comparisons (2005–2020)

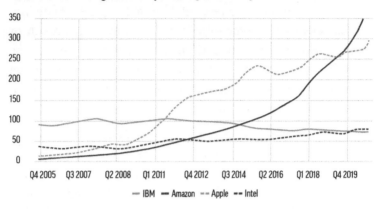

Source: Macrotrends

Figure 9 clearly depicts the faster growing revenues of Amazon and Apple, compared to IBM and Intel.

Now let's look at the stock prices. Figures 10 and 11 depict the stock prices for Apple and Amazon respectively over the same period.

**FIGURE 10:** Apple stock price (2005–2020)

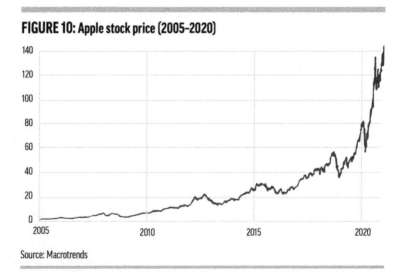

Source: Macrotrends

**FIGURE 11:** Amazon stock price (2005-2020)

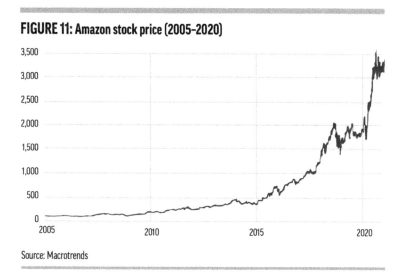

Source: Macrotrends

Figures 12 and 13 depict the IBM and Intel stock prices.

**FIGURE 12:** IBM stock price (2005-2020)

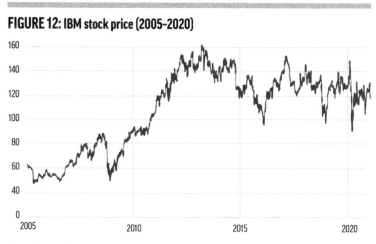

Source: Macrotrends

**FIGURE 13:** Intel stock price (2005–2020)

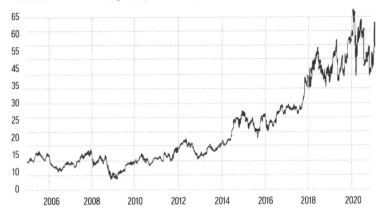

Source: Macrotrends

This simple analysis clearly shows how companies that continue to generate revenue growth have been rewarded with higher stock prices.

What is noticeable is that all the stock prices fell during 2018. Although there were other issues such as President Trump's US/China trade war, the main driving factor for this was the Federal Reserve raising interest rates, arguably too quickly for the stock market to digest.

If revenue growth drives stock price performance, then rising interest rates will create a reset in the stock prices and valuations.

## Characteristics of a growth stock

Let's now turn our attention to the characteristics of a growth stock, how we can compare apples with apples, how growth stocks are valued and what a technology expert likes to pay for growth companies.

As you have learnt, growth stocks typically exhibit high revenue growth, and as the business expands, grows and matures along the S curve, higher earnings growth rates should come through.

However, trying to compare and value growth stocks can be challenging, depending on where on the S curve the company is positioned.

First things first, though: growth stocks are typically valued and compared on the basis of future price-to-sales revenue. The price is the market capitalisation of the stock at any point in time and the future sales revenue growth refers to the year ahead. If the market capitalisation of a growth stock is US$200 billion and the current year's expected sales revenue is forecast at US$5 billion, then the price-to-sales ratio would be 200 divided by 5, equalling 40 times.

As the stock is yet to report bottom-line earnings growth, to justify a 40x multiple the company would be expected to show strong top-line (revenue growth) of at least 30 to 40% for the next two to three years. Investors would also look for other improving financial metrics such as higher customer growth and retention, higher margins and signs that cash flows will grow sufficiently to enable the company to report profits in the future.

In a low interest rate world, investors are happy to pay up for growth, as long as the revenue growth can be maintained. But how does revenue growth vary depending on the age of a company?

### Listing in a bull market

In bull markets, as witnessed in 2020 and 2021, the pick-up in the number of IPOs (initial public offerings or newly listed companies) is brisk. Unlisted companies will always seek out the best stock market conditions in which to raise equity. Listing the company allows growth companies to raise money cheaply (valuations are high, so less stock needs to be issued to raise the same amount of capital) and often founder stockholders can release some of their equity in the business. Bull markets in general will attract lots of new listings.

The current 2020–2021 bull market is no different in terms of investor appetite for new growth stories. We have witnessed a few high-profile names such as Airbnb coming to the market. However, a new listing can raise issues about comparing and valuing growth stocks or, put simply, comparing apples with apples and not apples with oranges.

For example, when a stock such as Snowflake (an enterprise data cloud service provider) listed in 2020, the company was seven years old and touted as generating the highest revenue growth ever for a software-as-a-service business. Snowflake was not only one of the most sought-after IPOs but it also became a bellwether for a change in stance from the legendary Warren Buffett, who took a large stake in the company pre listing. It is also arguably the most expensive growth stock on the market, valued at some 100x forward price-to-sales.

When you are looking at investing in growth stocks, particularly with the capital-light structures of software and cloud services, it is important you consider:

► The age of the company; and

► The rate of revenue growth relative to the age of the business.

What do I mean? The age of a company and the rate of growth are interconnected. Younger companies typically start out with a smaller revenue base. The smaller the base, the easier it is for management to grow the revenue.

For example, if a new, cloud-based software-as-a-service company is well sought after by the market (i.e. there's strong demand), the company can easily grow revenue over 100%, as doubling from US$1 million to US$2 million, for example, is easy.

Over time, as the revenue base grows, the rate of growth slows. It is considerably harder to double a revenue base from $100 million to $200 million than from $10 million to $20 million.

By definition, the larger and more successful the software product is, the more competition it attracts and the harder it becomes to grow and compete in the marketplace.

Although I have used software companies as the example, the same concept would apply to most start-ups. Henry Ford didn't move straight to mass vehicle manufacturing from day one.

## Maintaining revenue growth

Growth companies will be rewarded with a higher stock price as long as the revenue growth runways are maintained and the profit margins improve. Younger companies such as Snowflake, which are generating over 100% growth in revenue each quarter, year-on-year, have been valued at eye-wateringly high valuations. Depending on your risk tolerance and understanding of a company such as Snowflake, you can decide whether paying up to 100x market cap to future sales is justified.

With the proliferation of newly listed companies, particularly in the technology and software sectors, you need to keep an eye on how large the free float for the company is – meaning, are there enough shares listed to satisfy demand? In the case of Snowflake, the stock is tightly held between major stockholders as well as Salesforce and Berkshire Hathaway. The lack of available supply of stock to buy often inflates the stock price and thus the company's valuation. When the stockholders sell down, which often occurs over a period of time, that is usually a buying opportunity, all things being equal.

## Treasury bonds and growth stocks

So far you have gleaned that growth companies can receive high valuations if they are successfully generating high, year-on-year revenue growth. As they move along the S curve, their earnings growth should follow. You have also learnt that interest rates, and by default the US bond markets, have an impact on how stocks perform and how they are valued.

What you are probably not aware of is that, over the last five years, growth stocks have increasingly been priced as bonds.

As Bradley Krom Director Research at WisdomTree states:

> 'The analogy between bond returns and growth stocks is that total returns in the bond market are being driven overwhelmingly by price returns, as opposed to income.'

As interest rates have fallen to record lows, the concept of investing in treasury bonds has changed from buying the bond for income (the yield or the coupon) to buying the bond for capital gain.

Let me explain this in more detail. Put as simply as possible, a bond is issued by the U.S. Department of Treasury with a set start price, a fixed coupon or yield (interest payment per annum) and a redemption price (the price bond holders will be repaid by Treasury upon its maturity). Some bonds are 'short dated' (2-year treasury bonds) and some are 'longer dated' (10-year treasury bonds).

As the bond has a fixed coupon (interest payment) over the term of its life (which is also fixed), the price of the bond will be the component to change. If the Federal Reserve moves interest rates (the Fed funds) down, then bonds on issue with a higher yield will become more attractive to savers and investors. As the coupon (yield) is fixed, the investors will push up the price of the bond. Bonds are issued at what is called 'parity', so the price traded after issue will move around the parity price.

The more investors there are who want to buy the bonds, the higher the price rises and the lower the yield on the bond becomes. As interest rates have declined so considerably and the yields have been driven down, the prime driver of performance has been the increase in the bond price.

Growth stocks are similar, as they are at the earlier growth stages of their S curve and do not declare earnings or dividends. Therefore, like a bond, the growth in revenue is rated as a rise in the stock price. Growth stocks deliver a return through capital gains (stock price rises) not from income like the more traditional cyclical and value stocks.

As interest rates fall (normally because economic growth is subdued and cyclical stocks are not making good future earnings) investors gravitate to growth stocks.

Conversely, investors rotate into value cyclical stocks if there is an expectation of interest rates rising, which is usually a signal that economic growth is picking up and the cheaper stocks will benefit from improved business activity.

You will learn more about how interest rates impact on valuations of stocks in Chapter 9, as this is just one aspect of the story.

## Paying up for growth

How much growth should you pay up for? This is a good time to pivot to the technology expert and investor Beth Kindig. Ms Kindig has a phenomenal understanding of technology companies, having worked at Silicon Valley tech start-ups before honing her skills in how to invest in technology stocks.

One of the biggest hurdles to investing in newer growth stocks is the lack of historical earnings or background context to draw upon. Most investors look to the past performance of a company to ascertain what can be expected in the future, assuming management and leadership are retained and the markets the company operates in stay broadly similar.

This approach cannot be applied to newer companies, recently listed technology IPOs or change-makers such as Tesla.

As we have touched on, the price-to-sales ratio is a measure often used to establish how cheap or expensive a growth stock is to buy.

The first question we need to ask ourselves, when we're working out how much to pay for a growth stock, is 'What level of revenue growth is the stock generating?'

Beth Kindig has a number of categories defined as follows:

| Growth category | Revenues (yoy growth) | Example stocks |
|---|---|---|
| High Growth | Greater than 55% p.a. | Zoom, Twilio, Datadog |
| Medium Growth | Between 40 to 55% p.a. | Shopify, Tesla |
| Low Growth | Below 40% p.a. | Google, Facebook |
| Blended Growth | Moves between lower and higher growth | Apple |

Before we discuss at what price-to-sales valuations to buy stocks in these growth categories, it is important to dwell on the fact that high-growth companies cannot stay unprofitable forever. The stock market is happy to accept high growth revenue for a period, but ultimately the market wants to take comfort in the fact that the company will generate enough cash flow to cover not only investment for future growth, but also bottom-line earnings.

There was a clear example of this with Netflix's earnings announcement in January 2021. The company's stock price was rerated by over 20% after the company announced it was reaching the stage of positive-cash-flow generation (after the massive investments needed to produce streaming content) to declare earnings and eventually stock buybacks.

Investors cheer such developments, as the more self-sustaining a growth company can be (meaning there is enough free cash flow being generated to cover capital-expenditure commitments), the less the company has to rely on debt. There is nothing wrong with debt, particularly when interest rates are extremely low: the issue is always whether a company can service the debt and how impacted the company will be by rising interest rates.

## Timing the buying opportunities

As high-growth stocks are generally perceived as expensive, when is the right time to buy them from a valuation perspective?

Ms Kindig is generous enough to offer her opinion and, while you may decide never to invest in growth or to develop your own valuation methods or trading concepts, I believe the following suggestions are worthy of attention.

During rotational sell-offs, medium- to high-growth stocks – as outlined by the growth levels presented in the table opposite – will offer value around 20 to 30x forward (future forecast) price-to-sales.

In bull markets, these valuations can rise up to 50x price-to-sales and as much as 100x price-to-sales in some stocks, such as Snowflake. On such a high valuation, there is little room for disappointment and the stock could fall heavily if future revenue growth fails to meet expectations.

In the same way as value or cyclical stocks with more mature businesses are very sensitive to earnings downgrades or missing forecast earnings, growth stocks are very sensitive to the top-line revenue results. In terms of lower forward price-to-sales valuations of below 20x, Ms Kindig observes that a lower valuation is usually indicative of a value trap, where the company may not be the best in its field or has some issues that will impact its future growth. The metrics may alter if interest rates move higher than was anticipated. What seemed good value at 20 to 30x could well be compressed to 10 to 20x in a rising interest rate environment. Remember, most financial markets tend to over-compensate in both the sell-offs and the blow-offs (down and upside).

The point I am making is that whether it is a growth or value stock, it will have a range of valuations between which it will trade and, often, the valuations will change depending on the macro-economic backdrop (such as inflation and interest rate expectations) and what earnings, sales and margin expansion the business can achieve.

## Taking a look at tech

Before summarising the chapter, I want to highlight how the tech giants have moved from high-growth companies to value-growth companies. Although experiencing a new era of growth from 5G technology and the growth in service volumes, Apple now trades at a more market-based PER multiple of 27x forward earnings. Google is similar at 28x forward earnings. Both are still priced a little above the S&P 500 forward PER of around 23x – but not by much.

Apple and Google are also more expensive on a PER multiple than IBM and Intel (with PERs of 11.1x and 12.6x, respectively). But they trade well below Amazon and Salesforce at above 60x PER.

The bottom line is, your actions will depend upon your perspective and narrative. For example, if you only buy cheap stocks, then you would, by definition, only be looking at IBM and Intel, based on an expected improvement in earnings.

On the other hand, if you really believe in the tech giants, then you might be adding to these stocks during market pullbacks because you believe they can continue to grow their revenue and earnings through the economic cycles, as they have over the last two decades.

My point is that everyone, including the best experts, will subscribe to a narrative or a story that is in line with their views on the stocks and the macro-economic outlook.

As you will learn in the upcoming chapters, winning companies are usually defined by a set of characteristics that enable them to grow revenue and earnings over time.

## Chapter summary

- ► Secular growth businesses have the capacity to grow revenue and earnings irrespective of the macro-economic backdrop.

- ► Growth businesses often follow the S curve. The valuation of the stocks will vary depending on which stage the business is at on the S curve.

- ► Growth companies are often valued on a price-to-revenue or sales multiple. Valuations depend on the rate of future revenue growth relative to the past, and that is in correlation to the age and size of the company.

- ► Valuations are not static and will change over the course of a company's movement along the S curve. Growth companies can develop into value-growth and then value companies as the business matures.

# 6

# Secular megatrends: part two - growth sectors and stocks

Now it's time to take a deeper dive into the 21st-century megatrends.

Much has been written about how long these trends will last, particularly in light of the influence of COVID-19. You don't need me to tell you how your life changed in the 2020 pandemic year and, as we head into a vaccinated world, many of you might be asking whether your life will revert to the pre-pandemic normal. Or have our lives and the way we work, live and play changed irrevocably?

Those companies that successfully adapted to the pandemic will be asking the same questions. How will their businesses change as there is a return to (a new) normal?

You cannot underestimate the impact of the pandemic on those business models that were able to replace revenues with growth in sales from their online platforms. Many growth stocks experienced never-seen-before demand for their goods and services.

And, yes, I will go back to the Zoom example. We all took to the Zoom software like ducks to water to feed our hunger and need for social interaction, either at a personal level or as required by work. Zoom's revenue grew over 325% in 2020 year-on-year (yoy). Analysts described the revenue growth as 'pulled through' from future years, inferring that the lockdown conditions encouraged demand that would otherwise have taken longer to materialise in a pre-COVID economy. The 'pull through' trend can be seen across multiple online/digital sectors, including ecommerce.

The third decade of the 21st century will bring some of the greatest changes many of us will see. The risks and opportunities laid bare during 2020 are set to continue. However, if we look closely at the money trail, we will see that some major secular megatrends are only just beginning, meaning this decade could ring in the biggest investment opportunities in our lifetimes.

Let's look at those megatrends and the stocks in those sectors to shed some light on where the growth this decade might be found.

## Where are the money-making stocks?

Following is a list of secular-growth galaxies you could point your telescope towards. The list is not exhaustive of all the emerging trends, however, as regrettably too much has changed to cover in one chapter. You can do your own research and discover trends that I don't cover here or may not have covered in enough detail for your liking.

I have selected a group of themes that are easy for the retail investor to understand and I discuss some stocks in those sectors to provide some context for you. In some emerging industries, such as genomics, very few retail investors will have the expertise to understand the science behind the stocks, so I believe some sectors (such as genomics) should be left to the experts (more on how you can invest with the experts and through ETFs in Chapters 7 and 8).

So, what are some of the megatrends and do they have the potential to produce FAANMG (Facebook, Amazon, Apple, Netflix, Microsoft and Google) – like global giants if the forecasts come to pass? Let's take a look at:

- **Digital consumer transformation** – ecommerce (marketplaces), entertainment (gaming, gambling, streaming), telehealth and digital health, restaurant and food delivery, online fitness
- **Fintech** – digital wallets and payment systems
- **Cloud and edge computing** – data analytics, AI or machine learning, robotics
- **Clean energy and electric vehicles**
- **Other** – alternative foods, cannabis, space travel – 'to infinity and beyond'.

## Digital consumer transformation

Digital consumer transformation is an enormous mega-secular growth trend. The title has been sourced from the expert research team at Cowen Research Themes 2021.

The effect of digital disruption is pronounced across every aspect of our lives. While it has been estimated that the pandemic has pulled forward consumer demand by as much as six years in some instances, the expert research houses and institutional investors continue to forecast long-term growth runways.

We will now look at some of the major sectors within this megatrend.

## Ecommerce

We have touched on ecommerce a number of times in previous chapters, but the extent of the potential upscaling in this sector is probably underestimated. Even when the consumer has been unaware, human ingenuity has time and again been able to create new services and business concepts that become mainstream.

From humble beginnings as a disruptive online bookseller out of Jeff Bezos' garage, Amazon has evolved into a US$1.6 trillion company. As Jeff steps down in early 2021 as the CEO of Amazon, it is worth reflecting on just how far the world has come since the late 1990s.

> 'This journey began some 27 years ago. Amazon was only an idea, and it had no name. The question I was asked most frequently at the time was 'What's the internet?'. Blessedly, I haven't had to explain that in a long while.'

Amazon's growth spans two major secular themes: ecommerce and cloud computing (which contributes roughly 50% to earnings). The ecommerce division is no slouch and has created what is referred to by Professor Scott Galloway as 'rundles'. A rundle is when income is built around a bundled subscription service model. The Professor cites the success of Amazon Prime, a subscription-based marketplace of bundled goods and services including foodstuffs, clothing, streaming of movies and TV shows, and pharmaceutical prescriptions, all with the benefits of free, fast shipping for eligible purchases.

Establishing a rundle, or recurring revenue stream, for this business involved substantial capital investment in infrastructure and technology. Amazon has gone as far as buying second-hand aircraft, developing robotic warehouses and autonomous EVs to bypass incumbent transport and delivery services. However, rundles are increasingly the go-to business model for investors, as the income or revenue streams remain steady. Just think how challenged most of us are to change a longstanding subscription.

As you will find, subscription models across many digital platforms are growing apace and the valuations given to those stocks are higher, due to the perceived reliability and defensive nature of the earnings streams. Stock markets like certainty and bundled subscription services provide almost annuity-style incomes for normally cyclical business models.

### Digital marketplaces

The marketplace concept brings together the ultimate one-stop-online shop. With businesses like Amazon Prime, is it any wonder the traditional bricks-and-mortar operators are suffering?

Cathie Wood's ARK Invest has done some eye-opening research on the expected demise of bricks-and-mortar retailing in the USA. ARK expects that delivery drones will help drive the shift online by delivering packages for as little as 25c per trip (although, I am not too sure about buzzy drones whirling over my house).

> 'In our view, as a percent of retail, global e-commerce will quadruple from 16% in 2019 to 60% in 2030 as drones add to its convenience. As a result, retail real estate values are likely to suffer.
>
> 'ARK estimates that US e-commerce will grow from $820 billion in 2019 to $2.7 trillion in 2025, pushing non-e-commerce retail down from $4.6 trillion to $3.9 trillion, a level last seen in the late 90s.'

If you are an investor in bricks-and-mortar retail property trusts, the ARK Invest forecasts might give you reasonable cause to consider what investment risks lay ahead and how you should position your exposure.

The concept of the marketplace has been dramatically overhauled and changed by cloud-based digital disruption. There are new marketplaces popping up, including on Facebook and even the popular Pinterest. The Canadian Shopify is a winning growth story for providing a one-stop software-as-a-service to help new businesses create their digital presence. As its website attests: 'Bring your business online – create an ecommerce website backed by powerful tools that help you find customers, drive sales, and manage your day-to-day'. Anyone from anywhere in the world can use Shopify to create their online ecommerce presence via the Shopify services, software and marketplace.

Shopify's success is described by some analysts as one of the best 'product to market fits'. This is a term that describes the type of stock you want to own in any secular trend – the leaders with the best product that fits the market's needs.

## Digital entertainment

### *Online gaming*

Let's start with online gaming, a market Morgan Stanley estimates has 2.6 billion gamers globally and generated $135 billion in turnover in 2019. The pandemic has only increased demand and, with the rollout of 5G and mobile gaming, the market is expected to grow to $196 billion by 2022.

Online gaming exists on and is supported by numerous hardware platforms, including mobiles, TVs, the PC and the console – notably Microsoft's Xbox.

Improved technologies, including cloud gaming, will allow users to create their own content and play online in virtual or augmented reality. The improved speed of the 5G broadband should see an increase in mobile gaming to 50% of total sales in the next two years. In-game purchases (where the gamer is able to make real and virtual purchases through a game) are expected to drive more growth.

ARK Invest estimates 'revenue from virtual worlds will compound 17% annually from roughly US$180 billion today to US$390 billion by 2025'. Recently listed technology/virtual-reality gaming company Roblox is a case in point.

There remain ethical concerns about whether online gaming leads to, promotes or influences real-life behaviour (particularly in younger players), so it is reasonable to assume at some point there might be increased regulation in the sector.

The large players in the online gaming sector include the Xbox and Xbox 360 console-provider Microsoft; Zynga, a provider of social media and gaming services; and then the larger content gaming developers: Activision Blizzard (*Call of Duty*); Take-Two Interactive (*Grand Theft Auto*); and the unlisted Epic Games (*Fortnite*).

### Online gambling

Recently listed stocks DraftKings® and fuboTV are part of the new generation of digital entertainment, comprising online gambling, an online casino and online live sports betting.

The pandemic has changed the dynamics and even the regulatory environment, with some US State Governors (such as the Governor of New York, Andrew Cuomo) cutting red tape and allowing for online gambling. In part, the change is to offset the decline in gambling revenues from on-premises casinos, such as those owned by the Wynn Resorts and MGM (think Las Vegas or Atlanta).

DraftKings® is one of the lead companies expected to benefit from the growth in online gaming (gambling). Loop Capital considers the TAM (total addressable market) to be as much as $30 billion, double what another Wall Street analyst expects.

With the $36 million investment in the flamboyant Dave Portnoy's Barstool Sports company, Penn National Gaming (a casino owner and operator) has made a strategic decision to capture a share of the online gaming market. Barstool Sports is one of the largest (privately held) online sports betting companies and Portnoy became even more well-known for his stock trading ideas during the pandemic with Robinhood investors (the zero-cost trading platform).

Online gaming and online casinos will coexist alongside the bricks-and-mortar casinos. It will be interesting to see, once the COVID-19 virus is more under control, how quickly Americans race back to their beloved gaming venues.

A smaller and higher risk investment sports streaming service (or what the tech industry calls an OTT media or 'over the top content' company), fuboTV, has taken a step further to blur the lines between live sports streaming, online sports betting or gambling and free-to-play, fantasy gaming.

The free online gaming app is intended to help drive consumers to become subscribers to the streaming video platform and ultimately the sportsbook. The aim is for sportsbook wagers to become an enhancer of subscribers and user engagement, thereby earning higher revenues and lowering the customer acquisition cost.

OTT media is subscription video on demand (SVOD) via multiple platforms (personal computers, apps on mobiles or tablets and smart TVs). It bypasses pay TV and cable networks. Live sports, which fuboTV offers, is the latest of the 'cord-cutter' segments, referred to as such because viewers transition to them from cable and traditional pay TV services.

Roku is an interesting example of a disrupter of traditional media, as well as of the SVOD entertainment space. Video on demand is far from new and is becoming a more mature business segment, with the likes of Apple TV, Amazon Fire TV, Google TV and Chromecast and even Netflix and Disney+.

Roku, however, is perceived by some investors as a disrupter, and the service is rated highly by users because it possesses the largest channel selection. It also has the best operating system and connects with any smart TV via the Roku streaming stick, as well as multiple other mobile devices.

Roku's advantage is thought by some experts to be the fact that it has the best product in market for the consumer. With the best product in market, Roku is going to attract more advertising dollars – 'the dollars follow the eyes'. There is an increasing trend for advertising spend to move from the traditional pay channels, such as cable and satellite, to a Roku platform, where the spend can be more effectively targeted to audiences via the data sourced from each customer.

Other stocks that stand to benefit from the growth in global digital advertising spend include Google, Facebook, Pinterest, Snapchat and a newly listed stock called Magnite. According to Beth Kindig, advertising spend is forecast to grow 61% in the next four years to US$424 billion (from US$70 billion in 2011) and reach 61% of the total advertising spend by 2024.

I have mentioned DraftKings®, fuboTV and Roku to provide examples of how disruption remains a constant in the stock investing world, even when the newcomers are nudging up against some of the stock giants.

### Telehealth and digital medicine

Social distancing and containment of the spread of the coronavirus during 2020 resulted in a massive uptake in patient–doctor video visits, with 80% of US physicians using telehealth to consult with their patients versus 22% in 2019. Cowen Research expects this percentage to rise to 92% and remain there in the future.

Telehealth and digital health services cut across all aspects of the delivery of medical services and products, from general health to health insurance, second and expert opinions, chronic health care management and behavioural health.

Hefty health care costs in the United States and globally, as well as aging demographics, make the health care sector ripe for digital disruption.

Robotics and increased use of machine learning, as well as data analytics, will play a large role in diagnostic and surgery services. Nvidia (the digital chipmaker) highlighted at the J.P. Morgan Health Care Conference the tremendous role machine-learning applications (using chips) would have in all aspects of the health care and medical industry, including diagnostics, imaging, drug chemistry, genomics, pathology and biomedicine.

According to Beth Kindig, there are also substantial private equity funds flowing into the digital telehealth sector. Amwell and Teladoc are two of the major listed telehealth stocks. Australia's ResMed, with its dual Australia and US listing, is devoting resources to improved digital health solutions for its customers, using both cloud-based data and developing data analytics.

The sector remains very fragmented but has the potential to offer great money-making opportunities. Some investors were able to realise these when the online digital diabetic specialist Livongo was acquired by Teladoc in the second half of 2020.

Although *Shareplicity 2* is not touching on biotechnology and genomics stocks, I would be remiss not to mention that these sectors are also high growth. However, analysing these specialty sectors and stocks is probably best left to the experts. As a rule of thumb, the high failure rate in biotechnology makes for higher risk investments. (In Chapter 7, I discuss more ideas of how to invest in this sector via ETFs.)

## Restaurant and pick-up delivery

You only have to experience the shopping behaviour of gen Z to know there is growth for the recently listed DoorDash, or the incumbents Uber Eats and Grubhub.

While the older demographics were happy to have the occasional family pizza delivered, the younger generation are more than willing to spend a few dollars regularly if they don't have to leave the house or office for their favourite food or beverage.

## Online fitness

The last of the digital consumer sectors I'm profiling is online fitness.

With the global rollout of vaccines, there is a lingering uncertainty as to whether the growth rates of the stay-at-home, work-from-home stocks can be maintained, such as the exponential demand for the Peloton bikes.

However, only time will reveal whether we will embrace a love of crowded gymnasiums again.

According to the CEO of vaccine developer Moderna, Stéphane Bancel, at the J.P. Morgan Health Care Conference held in January 2021, 'SARS-CoV-2 is not going away'. The virus is expected to become an epidemic disease, meaning it will remain present or become present in communities forever, although the hope is that this will, be at lower levels as herd immunity and vaccines slow the disease.

Although no one knows for sure, trends such as online fitness have the potential for further growth runways. Peloton was one of the main 2020 beneficiaries, experiencing a 136% increase in connected subscriber growth in the September 2020 quarter.

Apple and other tech giants see the move to digital online health and fitness as a tremendous growth sector. Apple iPhone and Watch users would already be aware of the health-related apps available.

## Fintech

It's not often that Australia has a leader in the fintech world of innovation, but arguably the buy-now-pay-later company Afterpay is an example of the disruption that can be made to payments systems. Afterpay has joined the ranks of incumbent and recently US-listed Affirm and the Swedish behemoth Klarna.

Put simply, fintech is applying digital disruption to traditional banking and financial services models, most notably with what are referred to as 'digital wallets' or providing all your banking needs via the mobile or smart phone in your pocket or handbag.

According to ARK Invest, China has led the world in mobile payments, where growth has increased 15-fold in the last 5 years. Mobile payments now represent an estimated 3.5x China's GDP. Big names such as WeChat Pay and Alipay are synonymous with the growth in this market.

Latin American countries are also ready adopters of fintech, as trust around traditional banking and financial institutions is not high – think about the multiple banking crises that have afflicted their economies.

In the USA, research from ARK Invest suggests current digital wallets average between US$250 and US$1900 per wallet, but have the potential to scale to as much as US$20,000 per user. With scope for as many as 230 million US users in the future, the market could reach US$4.6 trillion by 2025.

As ARK Invest reports:

> 'Square's Cash App and PayPal's Venmo each amassed roughly 60 million active users organically in the last 7 and 10 years, respectively, a milestone that took J.P. Morgan more than 30 years and five acquisitions to reach.'

Combining technology and online digitalisation to facilitate lower cost, more transparent and easier accessibility to transactions, lending, payment systems and products on a mobile phone will eventually wipe out the need for bricks-and-mortar bank branches. But you didn't need me to remind you of this, as you have probably noticed how many fewer bank branches and how much less cash use there is in 2021.

Equally, the ecosystems fintech has created enable the digital providers to lower the cost of new customer acquisition and cross-sell their products.

Jamie Dimon, CEO of JPMorgan Chase, has been quoted as saying the banking and financial services giant should be frightened of fintech rivals, particularly in the payment space. The names he highlighted were Square (Cash App), PayPal (Venmo), Stripe and Ant Financial as well as the tech giants Amazon, Apple and Google. Walmart has also signalled its intention to move into the fintech payment space to evolve its business model as more of a one-stop-shop for customers.

## SPAC-tacular

While we are discussing disruption in the financial services sector, it is worth touching briefly on SPACs or special purchase acquisition companies.

The bull market conditions have encouraged not only a rush of new listings (IPOs), but also a rush by major 'expert' investors (normally billionaires) to raise money through listing a cash box, referred to as a SPAC.

The SPAC vehicle, in turn, looks for investment opportunities and acquires unlisted companies. The SPAC model allows companies to attain a stock listing without having to jump through some of the more onerous and vigorous requirements of the Securities and Exchange Commission's (SEC) IPO process.

The lack of regulatory oversight from the normal authorities also raises concerns that some of the companies acquired may not be as up to investment grade as the SPAC operators would like you to think.

SPACs are definitely more speculative and higher risk. That does not mean there won't be good opportunities, but as with many bull-market phenomena, the lack of substantial historical numerical data makes good investment risk analysis challenging. Do you remember the findings from Professor Bessembinder's research? Always keep in mind that most companies will not survive the long term and be real wealth-creators.

Before jumping into the SPAC market with all your hard-earned savings, it is definitely worth doing your research. Check out the governance of the SPAC creator, founder and CEO, as well as the work history of the new management of the acquired company.

In the fintech space, I came across one of the most interesting disruption models in the sector. The company is called SoFi, an abbreviation of 'social finance', and it was recently valued at in excess of $8 billion – so it's small relative to the banking and finance giants, however the business model is interesting.

SoFi started in 2011 as a student loan refinancing business and has since become a full-service financial product membership platform (a marketplace offering lending, deposit-taking and investment and insurance products). Its goal is to deliver full transparency, using an online platform providing lower cost financial and lending services to a market that often struggles with high-cost loans and securing finance. The membership model allows SoFi to add new services and products, such that 24% of new products come from existing members.

The SPAC that acquired SoFi is called Social Capital Hedosophia Corp. V, which is backed by venture capitalist Chamath Palihapitiya, who has brought companies like Virgin Galactic to the stock market.

SoFi is just one small example of the ever-evolving and growing space for digital fintech companies.

## Cloud and edge computing

The odd feature about perceived new trends is that they are, more often than not, former trends that for various reasons didn't take hold. Electric vehicles have been around since the transition from the horse and buggy, but it took over 100 years for technology to advance sufficiently to a level where the costs would compete with oil combustion engines.

While cloud computing is not that old, the origins of the concept are debatable. I was interested to learn from the Australian fund manager Roger Montgomery that in 2002, IBM's CEO, Louis Gerstner, wrote about the concept of 'utility computing'. Mr Gerstner's vision was to create an internet service for enterprises that would allow companies to outsource and decentralise all their information technology (data storage, processing, management systems and security) needs to a specialised computing utility.

However, the concept and description of what we now call the 'cloud computing' sector seem to have developed more in 2006 and 2007 with the growth of Google and Amazon.

The industry is dominated by three tech giants: AWS (Amazon Web Services), Microsoft via Azure and Google. In 2020,

Statistica estimated that AWS had 33% market share, followed by Azure with 18% and Google Cloud with 9%. All of the giants offer comprehensive services and products to transition businesses to and run them from the cloud.

The cloud function allows all of you to work from any device and location, using multiple software applications. The rise in demand has been supported by the lower costs and higher efficiency of internet and computing services provided by the cloud. When combined with the very cheap cost of capital, anyone can start a company without the substantial investment in inhouse IT and hardware that was needed only 15 years ago.

Walter Price at Allianz Global Investors cited Amazon as his top FAANMG stock in September 2020 on CNBC, due to the dominance of AWS in the sector and the tailwinds of its growth. By his estimate, still less than 5% of the global workload is on the cloud. This provides some context to the potential runway of growth opportunities for this sector.

Even though the software-as-a-service (SaaS) segment is the largest and growing strongly, as highlighted by expert investor Walter Price, the entire cloud market has massive growth potential, including the platform-as-a-service (PaaS) and infrastructure-as-a-service (IaaS) segments (see details following). The growth in cloud computing will be supported and enhanced by improved processing capabilities, touted by some to happen through considerable disruption to the major player semi-conductor company, Intel (x86 chip), with smaller, faster chips from ARM, TSCM (Taiwan Semiconductor Manufacturing Company) and the open source technology (meaning the technology is available to everyone free of charge) RISC-V.

The bottom line for investors is cloud computing will continue to grow as businesses realise the cost savings and efficiency improvements from not running their own inhouse IT departments, as well as substantial improvements in the processing power of data centres.

In Australia, you may be familiar with NEXTDC, the developer, owner and operator of cloud data centres. In the US, there are also a few major data centre property trusts (listed companies) that own the data centres. The largest is called Equinix, which owns and operates across the US and the rest of the world, including Australia.

The cloud market is basically split between three sectors:

1. **SaaS** – software solutions and services delivered digitally
2. **PaaS** – which allows for the development of software without the developers needing to worry about operating systems, software updates, storage or servers
3. **IaaS** – representing a virtual data centre, including all the infrastructure of data storage and servers; there is no need for maintenance and running costs.

## Software-as-a-service or SaaS

SaaS was one of the hottest investment themes for 2020. Some of the names that have been big winners for shareholders include Zoom (with its Programmable Communications Cloud software), Australia's Atlassian (enterprise software solutions), Workday (enterprise cloud applications for finance and human resources), ServiceNow (enterprise cloud-based solutions to improve workflow), CrowdStrike (cybersecurity cloud-based software), Cloudflare (cloud-based cybersecurity software) and Datadog (cloud-based IT software solutions).

It is also the sector seeing a plethora of new stock listings, including Databricks (enterprise cloud data processing) and UiPath (automated machine learning for enterprises).

Microsoft retains by far the biggest market share for enterprise (business) SaaS at around 16 to 17%, according to BMC Blog, followed by Salesforce with around 12%. Adobe, Oracle and SAP have another 20% between them and the next 10 smaller players have around 26%.

The SaaS model has also weaponised the profit model of software companies. For those of you who are old enough to recall, providers like Microsoft originally offered their software via a disk that you were required to buy at the same time as purchasing the hardware, then moved to offer the software as a download from their website. Both were one-off upfront revenue streams.

The SaaS model, in comparison, is based on a user-pays, subscription model accessed via downloadable software preprograms and services and is usually paid for in a monthly subscription. These models, like the rundle concept, allow for SaaS companies to be given a higher valuation, as customers tend to be stickier (meaning they just maintain the subscription) and revenue streams are regular and reliable.

Updates and bug fixes are also easily provided. How many times are you asked to download the latest software updates for your apps or Google Chrome and Microsoft Word or Excel?

There are no signs of the migration to the cloud abating over the long term. In some instances, there has been a slowdown in transitioning in some sectors due to the negative fiscal impact on companies from the pandemic, but many investors continue to view the cloud as a secular megatrend.

ARK Invest expects SaaS revenues to grow at an average compound rate of 21% p.a. until 2030, increasing the size of the market from revenues of US$100 billion in 2019 to around US$780 billion in 2030, or an 81% share of the total enterprise software market.

## Cybersecurity front and centre

The pandemic exposed some major risks from hackers and eCrime, particularly with many of us required to work from home.

eCrime is up some 330% since 2019. A major hack through the SolarWinds Orion software, a network software used by multiple US Federal government agencies and most Fortune 500 companies, allowed for malware to be installed into the systems of thousands of departments and companies. The hack was eventually found by a small cybersecurity company called FireEye that in turn notified SolarWinds. The fact that tech giants such as Microsoft and Cisco were attacked, as well as the biggest and most important US government agencies, laid bare how much risk of eCrime still exists.

Cybersecurity threats and prevention are top of the list of CEO concerns, as well as those of the Biden administration. Wedbush Securities analyst Dan Ives estimates there will be a 25 to 30% increase in incremental government spend as a result of the SolarWinds hack, and as much as US$200 billion in cybersecurity contracts up for the taking over the next two years. According to Mr Ives, cybersecurity is the go-to technology sector for 2021. The sector is also one of the most touted investment themes for the next decade.

Probably more confronting for investors is the number of stocks to pick from, as the sector is such a popular pick. There is a swath of old names (NortonLifeLock, McAfee, Palo Alto Networks and CyberArk software) and new cloud-based software companies to pick from, including CrowdStrike, Cloudflare, Okta, FireEye and then those companies with a particular exposure to Federal contracts, such as Telos, Zscaler, Tenable and SailPoint.

## Edge computing

Edge computing is being hailed as the new growth area in cloud computing. Edge computing simply means moving the computer servers (in the cloud) closer to the users to decrease latency response times (delays) and improve responsiveness and efficiency.

If the original cloud and digitalisation was for improving the work experience, efficiency and costs for humans and workplaces, then edge computing is for the burgeoning new growth industries of autonomous EVs, robotics and machine learning or AI.

This is the trend to which Viktor Shvets refers (quoted in the previous chapter), the transfer and acceleration in our economies of more goods and services being offered and provided by machines and computers.

Major players in the 5G theme include the telecommunications giants of Verizon and T-Mobile as well as Apple, Marvel, Qualcomm, Crown Castle and Skyworks.

Edge computing is as simple as it sounds. Have you noticed how long it can take to retrieve a file that is saved on the cloud? That is due to the fact that the server is located geographically a long way from your laptop or smart phone (in the cloud) and the broadband might be congested.

Now, imagine if you are using the full self-driving (FSD) function (as it is referred to at Tesla) for your EV in autonomous mode and the response time is delayed due to latency issues. By definition, the software cannot work as safely and efficiently as it needs to in order to provide a seamless and safe driving experience.

Edge computing will evolve and grow in line with the rollout of 5G wireless technology and networks, which are specifically designed to increase the speed and amount of content downloaded and made available to users. In turn, the technology will assist the machine-learning applications that industries are developing across multiple growth platforms, from drones to smart cities, robotics, autonomous EVs and data analytics.

Analysts expect a lot of competition in the edge computing and 5G sectors, with the major telephony giants of Verizon and Intel seeking to regain some market share and control.

If, at this stage, you are feeling somewhat overwhelmed with information, do not despair, as in Chapters 7 and 8 I will reveal how to invest in these sectors. You may also be starting to see how interlinked all these technology secular megatrends are. At the heart of most of the change is the technological disruption and disintermediation that is being allowed to evolve as a result of the faster innovation of software and hardware in the information and digital age.

## Clean energy and EVs

*'Climate change is the investment opportunity of our generation.'*

– Mark Carney, former governor of the Bank of England

It is hard to envisage that America, a country many of whose wealthiest families and billionaires made their fortunes from fossil fuel, namely oil, is now on the precipice of becoming a global leader in clean energy and electric vehicles.

This has been a sector on the verge of emerging for years and 2021 marks the start of what experts (and Shareplicity) believe will be a watershed moment in history, when the US starts to lead the world towards a net-zero-emissions target by 2050. That is the goal of President Biden's clean energy targets and incentivised investment programmes that aim to decarbonise the US economy.

The drive to transition away from fossil fuels has come about through substantial technological advances in alternative energy sources, such as renewables like wind and solar. This has lowered the costs dramatically, making clean energy competitive with traditional energy generation via coal, gas and nuclear.

Institutional investors have been spurred on to invest in clean energy by the moral objective of ever-greater ESG (environment, social, governance) investment flows. They also fear potential climate risk litigation from trustees of pension funds if they are left holding stranded fossil fuel assets.

Although all the secular growth themes are expected to produce companies that will maintain high growth rates and offer excellent investment opportunities, the winners in the clean energy area and in EV or zero-emission vehicles will be the greatest money makers for investors this decade.

Why? The answer is simple: decarbonising is the biggest challenge and change to business and society since the railways or the move from the horse and buggy to motorised vehicles. In 1900, a picture of the New York Easter Parade on Fifth Avenue showed all horse and buggy transport. By 1913, the Easter Parade had only one horse and buggy and the rest were motor vehicles.

Investors should never underestimate the rate of change when cascades of investment monies are looking for a return in a new sector.

Cowen Research estimates up to US$3 trillion a year will need to be invested to reach the global net-zero-emissions 2050 goal. Goldman Sachs forecasts green infrastructure spending of between US$1 trillion to US$2 trillion over the next decade in the US alone, doubling the size of the total addressable market.

As highlighted previously, the oil and the automotive markets are the two largest markets in the world. When you combine replacing these with replacing other fossil fuel energy supplies, it is hardly surprising that the potential inflows of capital decarbonising transport and energy are so mind-bogglingly humongous.

The total global economy (GDP value) was around US$88 trillion in 2019, according to the latest World Bank data, so Cowen is broadly estimating spending of around 3.4% per annum of total global GDP.

### Clean energy – solutions for net-zero-emissions

*'There is no company whose business model won't be profoundly affected by the transition to a net zero economy.'*

– Larry Fink, BlackRock, co-founder

CEO of SunPower, Tom Werner, cited that the cost of solar energy generation had declined by 82% since 2010 and that 92% of all new energy generation in 2020 was based on renewables.

UBS estimates energy storage costs will fall between 66 and 80% over the next decade and the value of the market will grow to US$428 billion.

I am pretty sure I have your attention now. There is a waterfall of money that will be looking to find a home in the best transition companies – and there are many to choose from on the US stock markets, which is great news for investors.

However, like the gold rush to internet stocks in the late 1990s and early 2000s, not all companies will be winners and the me-too copycats could lead many an investor astray.

Renewable energy is intermittent, meaning the sun doesn't always shine and the wind doesn't always blow when we need the electricity. Large-scale storage then becomes the enabler to capture the energy when it is produced and disburse the energy when it is needed.

The process also requires software to make the grids smarter to meet consumer demands.

Battery storage is the burgeoning growth area for reliable electricity grids and EVs. The cost, the rate and the magnitude of sustainable battery production hold the key to the decarbonising process being achieved at affordable levels and at scale. UBS estimates that battery storage costs will fall by up to 80% over the next decade and the value of the market will rise to US$426 billion in the US.

Tesla's goal to reduce the cost of lithium-ion batteries (the major source of batteries globally for a wide-ranging group of products, including our electronic devices – from smart phones to tablets, laptops and PCs) has made the cost of battery-powered cars competitive with some internal combustion engine (ICE) vehicles. The goal going forward is to reduce the cost further.

Renewables are not the only potential zero-emission technologies. Hydrogen fuel cells and green hydrogen (hydrogen produced by renewable energy) are part of the mix, along with a suite of other technologies, some more speculative and unproven than others.

### Electric vehicles or hydrogen vehicles?

Elon Musk's Tesla is held up as the leading light in EVs, but all major ICE manufacturers are now producing and expanding their electric vehicle production or hybrid (part-battery, part-gasoline) models. Hydrogen fuel cell cars are being developed in Korea and for more large-scale transport such as semi-trailers.

General Motors (GM) has pledged to make all its vehicles electric by 2035. If you are not surprised, then you should be. This is a 'gotcha' moment in history, when a major incumbent legacy car manufacturer will actively transition to zero-emission electric vehicles. If Elon Musk's goal was to kickstart the revolution, then on at least one count he can now tick the box.

GM's CEO and Chairman, Mary Barra, stated, 'Climate change is real, and we want to be part of the solution by putting everyone in an electric vehicle'.

Backing up those words is GM's commitment to invest US$27 billion in new manufacturing capabilities and battery plants over the next four years. This amount is well in excess of what is currently invested.

With the UK, Denmark, Ireland, the Netherlands, Slovenia, Israel, India and Sweden banning all new ICE vehicles from 2030, and France and Singapore after 2040, BloombergNEF (a specialised research division of Bloomberg) estimates that by 2040, 57% of new passenger car sales will be electric.

### Clean energy stocks to invest in

Chapter 7 outlines the ETFs available in this space, which I highly recommend, as there are many avenues to invest in to take part in the clean energy and electric vehicles revolution.

By this stage, you have probably worked out that I remain convinced that Tesla is a game-changer and leader in the sector. Its business cuts across many dimensions to bring affordable clean energy to the market, as well as affordable, smart electric vehicles.

Following in Tesla's footsteps is a suite of incumbent vehicle manufacturers who are tackling the transition challenge, as well as Chinese players such as NIO, XPeng, Li Auto and BYD (in which Warren Buffett's Berkshire Hathaway has invested).

There are numerous solar energy plays including Enphase, SolarEdge, Sunrun and First Solar, to name a few. NextEra Energy is the largest and most developed energy utility and, if you prefer to play the input materials, there are also the lithium suppliers, rare earths, copper and nickel producers.

Albemarle, the largest US lithium producer, has estimated that the demand for lithium will grow four-fold in the next five years. Many investors may decide to play the clean energy revolution via the mineral and materials sectors, but keep in mind these stocks are subject to the price vagaries created through changing demand and supply conditions.

## Other – robotics, alternative foods, cannabis, space

Robotics, alternative foods, cannabis and space represent some of the in-vogue secular themes, but always capturing a profitable investment in any of these sectors can be challenging. I will touch on all of them briefly as an outline for further possible ETF ideas.

The impacts of climate change, growing populations, water and land scarcity are driving a burgeoning industry of technological innovation in the food production sector. Whether it is due to the drive to alternative meat or protein sources – Beyond Meat is a leader in alternative meat products, a US$3 trillion market – or the development of indoor vertical gardens, I expect there will be emerging opportunities in this sector.

Bank of America refers to the future food market and lists a number of stocks that are involved in either the production, development or distribution of food sources, including the equipment giant Deere, food delivery services Uber and DoorDash and Amazon.

The cannabis sector is also expected to show good growth over the next decade, with Cowen expecting the market's revenue to double from around US$51 billion to US$100 billion by 2030.

Around 34% of the US population use cannabis for either recreational or medicinal purposes and, with the ongoing legalisation of the product in more US states, cannabis is one of the growth sectors for investors.

There is a suite of cannabis growers and suppliers, many of whom have been in the doldrums for years, who are now shining after the Biden victory, expecting a favourable stance to the sector. GrowGeneration Corporation, an interesting play, is an expanding retail chain of hydroponic and organic gardening stores in the US and is called the 'picks and shovels' of the sector. This tag harks back to the gold rush era when the people who made the most money from gold mining were the providers of the basic tools – picks and shovels. This is a very fragmented sector; growth is being achieved via both acquisitions and new site developments.

Like many commodity-based products, there is a low barrier to entry to cannabis production and it's generally a low-margin business. While US states are looking to legalise cannabis use to help fill the gap in state revenues, I remain predisposed to investing via expert fund managers.

Robotics and automation are undeniably major themes that cut across many sectors of our economies – from more automated warehouses for ecommerce to manufacturing. Robotics and automation bring forth a moral dilemma. The advances in these two technologies contribute to a dramatic shift in the way some industries operate, including in their data collection, analytics and processing, manufacturing, accommodation, food services and retail trade.

According a report by management consultant McKinsey, 'A future that works: Automation, employment and productivity' (2017), an estimated 50% of all the activities people are paid to do in the world could be potentially automated, representing US$15 trillion in wages. The US represents around 51% of the global workforce or US$2.7 trillion in wages.

The experts feel that humans will not be totally displaced but the workload will be considerably reduced by integrating robotics and automation into processes.

It is not hard to see that the pandemic has brought forward the move in this direction. How many of you started ordering groceries online in lockdown and are now continuing to do so? Once retail warehouses are automated, the costs for online shopping will drop for the suppliers, allowing for improved margins and profits.

Space themes are a reality with the SpaceX and Blue Origin companies of billionaires Elon Musk and Jeff Bezos. Space themes are not new but have been in a hiatus for many years with reduced fiscal government spending.

With financial backing and commitment re-emerging in the relative-to-history, lower-for-longer interest rate environment and an increased commitment to innovation, both supersonic travel and satellite internet are on the cards as a reality, according to founder and CEO of ARK Invest, Cathie Wood.

SpaceX is working on Starlink, with as many as 1000 satellites launched to date. Although you can't buy SpaceX yet, you can invest in Richard Branson's Virgin Galactic. This company is aiming to provide spaceflight for wealthy individuals.

Aerospace exposure also exists through some of the more traditional names of Boeing, Lockheed Martin and Northrop Grumman.

## The backbone of change

Chapter 6 would not be complete without briefly mentioning the semiconductor or chip design and manufacturing sector. Semiconductors are at the heart of all electronic devices. Traditionally, the industry was highly cyclical, as demand fluctuated for the end-use products, such as smart phones and cars.

However, with the growth in above-mentioned megatrends, those chipmakers supplying to the EV, gaming, cloud computing and robotics markets (companies like AMD and Nvidia) are expected to benefit.

Traditionally, the chips and semiconductors were a more commoditised market and dominated by big players like Intel. However, specialisation based on speed, size and graphics is allowing for stock differentiation.

## Chapter summary

- ► There is a large and growing number of secular megatrends that are changing the world.

- ► If history is anything to go by, most of us underestimate the rate of change and technological innovation.

- ► The secular growth markets and the companies that operate in those sectors will offer some big money-making ideas in the themes covered in this chapter.

- ► Investors can take advantage of these opportunities through investing directly in some of the stocks named in this chapter.

- ► Not all stocks will be winning investments in the secular megatrends.

- ► Exchange traded funds (ETFs) provide even more opportunities and may be better suited to your risk profile.

# 7

# Investing in the US indirectly via ETFs and ESG funds

By now I hope your introduction to secular megatrends has given you the confidence and inspiration to expand your investing horizon. If you are nervous about buying directly into a US stock listed on an overseas exchange, however, then you're not alone. I'm sure many investors are hesitant to take the first step. That's why this chapter is about starting to invest in US companies, but through an exchange traded fund. You may already hold Australian ETFs. If so, all the better: this won't be a big step at all.

As with stocks, not all ETFs are created equal, so in this chapter I take a more in-depth look into these financial products to help you navigate your way through both the risks and the opportunities they offer. In the second part of the chapter, I shine a light on environmental, social, governance (ESG) investing to give you more insights into how fund managers are constructing funds for the future.

Let's start with the basics and then run through the different types of ETFs.

## Back to basics

Exchange traded funds (ETFs) or exchange traded products (ETPs) are traded on the stock exchange. They are like the wrapper around a bundle of stocks or bonds that the ETF owns.

Jack Bogle, founder of Vanguard, is often considered the grandfather of ETFs. He most astutely explained:

> 'In investing, you get what you *don't* pay for. Costs matter. So intelligent investors will use low-cost index funds to build a diversified portfolio of stocks and bonds, and they will stay the course. And they won't be foolish enough to think that they can consistently outsmart the market.'

Vanguard's low-cost index funds were the forerunners to ETF financial products. Instead of buying into a managed fund that owned a selection of stocks that had been researched and selected by the fund managers, investors were able to buy a low-cost fund that mirrored the stocks of an index.

Do you recall the research from Professor Hendrik Bessembinder? He proved that most stocks do not outperform treasury bonds (let alone the stock market index). The findings are the same for active fund managers, the professional experts who raise money from you and me and invest the funds on our behalf. Many actively managed funds do not outperform the index they are investing in or their benchmark, after costs, for long periods of time – unless of course the benchmark is set very low.

It makes sense, when you think about the concept of active funds management. The manager has a mandate for the fund you buy into. The mandate might be to outperform the S&P 500 and the manager's investment style or factor might be 'value'.

However, the value style of investing, for numerous reasons, has underperformed the growth style since 2015. So, if you had invested in a managed fund comprising value stocks, you would have watched as growth stocks shot the lights out in terms of performance – think FAANMG (Facebook, Apple, Amazon, Netflix, Microsoft and Google) growth – while your value managed fund would have underperformed.

Active management is what some experts refer to as a zero-sum game, meaning not all fund managers can be winners all the time. Basically, every dollar of outperformance must be matched by an equal amount of underperformance. You only have to take a look at your own stocks to know that they do not all rise by the same percentage each day, week, month or year. Sadly, you (or any expert) cannot own all the winning or outperforming stocks all the time, or as Australian investor Claude Walker says, 'you can't pat all the fluffy dogs'.

What you can own is an investment product that allows you to keep pace with the stock market index or the sum of all the stocks in the index, including the stocks that outperform and the stocks that underperform. These are the constituents of an index and, by definition, the index will rise or fall depending on the composition of stocks.

If a stock market index rises by 10% p.a., you will double your money over seven years. Sounds easy, I know, but in reality, stock markets can be volatile (move up and down). As the legendary investor Warren Buffett says, 'it's not about timing the market but time in the market'.

One of the reasons financial planners and investors love ETFs is because buying an ETF takes the hassle out of picking the winning stocks and avoiding the losing stocks. You can just add more to your ETF holdings over time or switch themes or sectors as appropriate.

This sounds like a wonderfully simple and straightforward strategy and, in principle, the concept is sound. However, in order to establish an investment approach around ETFs, you first need to have an understanding of the types of ETFs that are available and what to look out for.

## Size of the global ETF market

The simplicity and ease of investing in ETFs, as they are traded on stock exchanges, has helped grow the number and value of products on offer. The value of ETF products has almost doubled in size every four years since 2005. The global industry is now worth over US$7 trillion and continues to take market share from the actively managed funds market. This is because the cost of the financial product (the ETF wrapper) is lower and performance has been better than the traditional actively managed funds.

The number of ETFs in the US has increased from 123 in 2003 to 2204 in 2020, according to Statistica, with an estimated value around US$5 trillion.

There are almost 7000 listed ETFs on global stock markets to choose from and each day more are being created and coming to market. You should never underestimate just how creative the world of finance is when it comes to feeding hungry investors with new financial products.

So, let's explore the different ETF products that are available and what the differences mean for you when you are making your ETF investment selection.

## Passive ETFs

The ETF product (representing the bulk of the ETFs on offer) was originally designed and sold as what the industry calls a 'passive' investment, which tracks an index, for example. It's 'passive' because the fund manager structures the ETF product to hold the underlying stocks that replicate the index the product is mandated to track. The fund manager is not overriding the weighting of the stocks in the index – they're not buying more Apple stock, for example, than the percentage amount Apple actually represents in the index on any one day.

The finance industry, however, being innovative and keen to offer you a new product that might sway you to part with more of your savings, decided to create ever more styles of ETFs. You can now buy sector ETFs – such as financials or energy or gold sector ETFs – and most recently there has been a deluge of what are called 'theme' ETFs, active ETFs and non-transparent active ETFs.

Let's look at each separately and keep in mind that the ETF industry is one of the fastest growing sectors of wealth management.

Theme ETFs are ETF products created to suit a narrative or theme, such as cybersecurity, EVs, cannabis, genomics, founder-run companies, video games and e-sports or infrastructure (we looked at some of these themes in the megatrends chapters). Usually, the stocks in the ETF are selected from an existing, predetermined index of stocks created by an agency to reflect the theme. In other instances, the fund manager selects the stocks in what is referred to as an 'active' ETF (more on this soon).

There is even a World Without Waste ETF designed to focus on companies that work on evolving a circular, not linear economy. JPMorgan released the Carbon Transition U.S. Equity ETF and Inspire Investing takes the screening and thematic process one step higher to God with biblically aligned stocks with high growth potential – the ticker code is FEVR if you want to check out the product. (We cover ESG ETFs later in the chapter.)

Pretty much any theme or income generation play is out there for you to choose from, including what are called 'bear/short' funds, which are designed to make you money when the stock markets sell off.

A word of caution on the proliferation of ETF products. Although ETFs offer easily accessible, long-term investment options, they are not immune from the irrational exuberance or greed that you may have witnessed in stock markets. ETF products can therefore benefit from too much liquidity and excessive optimism and price momentum. I recommend you adopt a prudent strategy when buying them, such as not chasing prices when everyone else is.

## Active ETFs

The ETF industry has increasingly moved to offer a product that is similar to the traditional actively managed funds but lower in cost, and these are referred to as active ETFs.

An active ETF allows the fund manager to actively (consciously) select the stocks and bundle them in an ETF product wrapper. As the fund manager has a more engaged role, the cost of an active ETF will be higher than a passive ETF, but below the cost of an actively managed fund like an investment trust. Until recently, active ETFs were legally required to announce the change in stock holdings daily, meaning anyone could find out what a successful fund manager was buying and selling. This meant retail investors could copy or try to copy the success of active ETF managers.

Although active ETFs only represent 3.5% of the US$ 5.7-trillion-pie, some active ETFs have had some stellar success.

Cathie Wood, CEO of ARK Invest (quoted widely in the previous chapter and famous for being one of the first and most outspoken supporters of Tesla) created actively managed ETFs that are now growing rapidly in popularity. No wonder: the ARK genomic revolution fund returned a shoot-the-lights-out 200% capital return in 2020, and the ARK Innovation ETF returned 170%.

The ARK Invest funds grew in size (from funds inflow and the underlying stock performance) from US$3.6 billion in 2019 to US$50 billion at the end of 2020. They have seen as much as US$11 billion inflow at the start of 2021. The growth in demand for the ARK funds underscores not only the increase in investor appetite for disruptive innovation stocks (many of which do not make any money) but the almost cultlike following of keen investors who tweet about what stocks the fund has been buying and selling. Cathie Wood is referred to as the 'Money-Tree' in Korea.

The Securities and Exchange Commission (SEC) regulated in 2019 that active ETFs could operate as semi- or non-transparent, meaning the manager does not have to reveal daily the stocks bought, sold and held. This means retail investors would not be able to jump on the bandwagon and chase the momentum of a successful fund manager.

In contrast to the commendable transparency of ARK Invest ETFs, it is more typical of traditional active fund managers to talk generalities rather than specific stock changes. Alternatively, they will discuss around the styles, themes and possible stock examples they like and for what reasons.

## Index and equal weighted

One last important aspect to appreciate with ETFs is how the stocks are weighted in the ETF. Consider two of the largest ETFs that aim to replicate the price and yield of the S&P 500:

1. **SPY** (SPDR S&P 500 ETF Trust) – the largest ETF by assets under management, with a market cap of US$350 billion and a 1.38% dividend yield

2. **IVV** (iShares Core S&P 500 ETF) – the second-largest ETF with a market cap of US$269 billion.

Both have Apple, Microsoft, Amazon, Facebook and Alphabet (Google's parent company) as the top holdings, representing 20% of the ETF. This means when you buy an index-weighted ETF, you need to understand what underlying stock prices will drive the performance of the ETF. With both of these ETF giants, you are buying into the performance of the tech giants. Should their stock prices fall, then the ETF will be disproportionally impacted by the performance of just six giant companies.

If there were a spike in inflationary expectations and a steep rise in the US 10-year treasury bond, it would not be unreasonable for the more expensive growth tech giants to be sold off and the flow of funds to switch into the more value/cyclical sectors and financials. If you weren't aware of this, you might wonder why the biggest ETFs started to stumble while other stocks in the S&P 500 were rising (e.g. Berkshire Hathaway and the banks, like JPMorgan, Wells Fargo and Morgan Stanley).

As usual, the ETF industry has come up with a solution and that is an ETF that tracks the stocks in the S&P 500 but gives each stock an equal weighting, not a market cap index weighting. One such ETF is Invesco's S&P 500 Equal Weight ETF (ticker code RSP). As all the stocks are equally weighted quarterly, the ETF removes what is referred to as the concentration risk (i.e. too much exposure in the ETF from a just few stocks).

## Costs matter

Discussion around active and passive ETFs is not complete without touching on costs. ETF providers charge a percentage of the amount you are investing as a fee. Passive funds can charge expense ratios as low as 0.02 to 0.03% and up to 0.10% is considered reasonable. The active ETFs will probably have higher expense ratios, as you are paying more for the fund manager to select the stocks, compared to a passive ETF. Actively managed funds charge fees of around 0.7% upwards and over 1%; 1.5% is considered expensive. The downward pressure on fees will continue as demand for ETFs increases.

## Money moves markets

By now you are probably thinking, 'Why does this all matter to me?' You just see stock markets going up and want to be part of the uptrend. Well, the reason is that money moves markets.

The bottom line is, when ETFs experience large capital inflows (as happened to ARK Invest), the operators of the ETF have to buy stocks to fulfil their investing mandate. If you happen to own the stock/s they are buying you may inadvertently be benefiting from a rising stock price related purely to the weight of money coming to the market from the ETF product.

The world's largest fund manager, BlackRock, estimates that ETF funds will reach US$12 trillion by 2023, and that would continue the historic trend of doubling the size of these products every four years.

My US portfolio undeniably benefited in 2020 from being part of a group of high-growth disruption and technology stocks that happened to appear in a number of ETF offerings. Is it any wonder that what is called the 'weight of money' factor is driving the valuations of certain themes and stocks?

You also need to understand that liquidity matters, not only for the ETF you are buying into (as in the size of the fund) but also for the underlying stocks the ETF holds. A prime example in 2020 was the entry of Tesla stock into the S&P 500, where the company went from a zero weighting to being the sixth-largest stock in the index.

Billions of dollars of funds from index-tracking ETFs and benchmark managed funds (these funds track the index too) had to buy Tesla stock. At the most basic level, finance is about the demand for and supply of stocks; more buyers than sellers and the prices go up, and vice versa.

One of the concerns about ETF products exists around the liquidity or the monies going into an ETF fund and the manager having to allocate the funds across stocks. If the liquidity in the underlying stocks is not high, and the funds raised continue to grow, the weight of money can exacerbate the increase in stock prices. The impact can also work to depress stock prices. A recent example of when an index was reweighted was reported in the *Australian Financial Review (AFR)*. Two small New Zealand stocks were adversely impacted by BlackRock's reweighting of the iShares clean energy ETFs.

It is easy to see how investor momentum and trends like the big secular themes can move stocks. But in the same way as they can push the stocks too high, they can equally cause the stocks to sell off aggressively.

This leads me to one of the most important aspects around investing in ETFs: you must understand what stocks are represented in the ETF wrapper.

Investing in ETF products is about understanding how different factors will underscore the momentum and flow of funds to the ETFs. As I write, the hot themes are around EVs, and investors are understandably drawn to the narrative. Electrification of the vehicle market is valued at US$2.5 trillion.

When too much money is looking for a home in the same theme, then overvaluation of the stocks and the ETFs in the theme inevitably occurs.

The message is always to keep your eye on what you are buying, why you are buying the ETF, what your investing horizon is and how you will react if there is a large shift in funds flowing away from the style, factor or theme of ETF you have invested in.

The finance industry likes you to think ETFs are safe and passive (implying no volatility) but don't be fooled. As with any stock or financial product, they can be subjected to irrational exuberance. Greed and fear of missing out (FOMO) can lead you to buy at the wrong time in the market cycle or in an industry that is just too speculative or interest-rate-sensitive, should inflation expectations and interest rates rise, for example.

## Local buying opportunities

I have given you an overview of ETFs and highlighted some of the red flags, but they are for most of us a great avenue to grow our wealth.

I approach structuring an ETF portfolio in the same way as I select stocks. First, I ask myself, 'What am I trying to achieve in buying this ETF?' Diversification is usually the key to constructing a robust ETF portfolio. The theory is that not all asset classes move together and if you invest in a diverse range of assets, you'll achieve long-term growth.

The second question you need to ask yourself is, 'Do I want to buy the ETFs in US dollars and on US stock markets or would I prefer to buy the US ETF products listed in Australia?'

The Australian suite of ETF products permits you to invest without having to worry about currency concerns (with the currency hedged ETFs) or the US's W-8BEN tax form – the IRS Certificate of Foreign Status of Beneficial Owner for United States Tax Withholding and Reporting (Individuals). However, the expense cost for some of the overseas themed Australian listed ETFs can be higher than their US counterparts. Costs such as currency hedging are likely culprits for the differential.

Let's start by looking at which ETFs with US exposure are available on the local Australian market (see Table 3).

**TABLE 3:** Australian ETFs with US exposure (in alpha order of ETF provider)

| Fund | Ticker | Global category |
|---|---|---|
| BetaShares Geared US Equity Fund – Currency Hedged | GGUS | Geared exposure to S&P 500 |
| BetaShares Strong US Dollar Hedge ETF | YANK | Alternative miscellaneous |
| BetaShares Global Energy Coms ETF – Currency Hedged | FUEL | Natural resources equity |
| BetaShares Global Cybersecurity ETF | HACK | Technology sector equity |
| BetaShares NASDAQ 100 ETF | NDQ | US equity large cap blend |
| BetaShares NASDAQ 100 ETF – currency hedged | NHDQ | Currency Hedged US equity large cap blend |
| BetaShares S&P 500 Equal Weight | QUS | S&P 500 Equal Weight Index |
| BetaShares S&P 500 Yield Maximiser | UMAX | US equity large cap blend |
| BetaShares US Equities Strong Bear Fund – Currency Hedged | BBUS | Generates returns negatively correlated to the S&P 500 index |
| BetaShares Climate Change Innovation ETF | ERTH | Tracks the Solactive Climate Change and Environmental Opportunities Index |
| Beta Shares Cloud Computing ETF | CLDD | Tracks the Global Cloud Computing Index |
| BetaShares Global Banks ETF – Currency Hedged | BNKS | Global equity large cap |
| BetaShares Global Income Leaders ETF | INCM | Global equity large cap |
| ETFS Morningstar Global Technology ETF | TECH | Technology sector equity |
| ETFS S&P 500 High Yield Low Volatility | ZYUS | US equity low-volatility high yield |
| ETFS Battery Tech and Lithium ETF | ACDC | Global equity large cap |
| ETFS Ultra Long Nasdaq 100 Hedge Fund | LNAS | Geared returns to the Nasdaq 100 |

| Fund | Ticker | Global category |
|---|---|---|
| ETFS Ultra Short Nasdaq 100 Hedge Fund | SNAS | Geared returns that are negative to the Nasdaq 100 |
| ETFS ROBO Global Robotics and Automation ETF | ROBO | Equity miscellaneous |
| ETFS Global Core Infrastructure ETF | CORE | Global equity large cap |
| MFG Core International Fund | MCSG | Global large cap |
| MFG Core International Fund | MCSI | Global infrastructure |
| MFG Core ESG Fund | MCSE | High quality global large cap |
| iShares Core S&P 500 | IVV | US equity large cap blend |
| iShares S&P 500 Currency Hedged | IHVV | US equity large cap blend |
| iShares Core S&P Mid-Cap 400 | IJH | US equity blended mid cap |
| iShares Core S&P Small-Cap ETF | IJR | US equity 600 small cap |
| SPDR S&P 500 ETF Trust | SPY | US equity blend |
| SPDR S&P Global Dividend Fund | WDIV | Global equity large cap |
| SPDR Dow Jones Global Real Estate ETF | DJRE | Real estate sector equity |
| Vanguard US Total Market Shares Index ETF | VTS | Market cap weighted CRSP US Total Market Index |
| VanEck Vectors Video Gaming and eSports ETF | ESPO | Tracks MVIS Global Video Gaming and eSports Index |
| VanEck Vectors Global Clean Energy ETF | CLNE | S&P Global Clean Energy Index |

Sources: Market Index, Bloomberg, Canstar, BetaShares, Morningstar

In Table 3, I have summarised the available ETFs that are listed in Australia to offer you an exposure to US stocks and themes (with a predominantly large US weighting) to help start you on your research pathway. This is a fast-growing sector in Australia and, barring any market meltdowns, I believe it is safe to assume the offering to Australian investors will continue to increase over time. The thematic ETFs are very attractive to younger investors who are keen to establish a position in those companies and sectors that they believe are good long-term wealth-making opportunities.

As you can see from the selection in the table, you can achieve exposure to many of the themes we discussed earlier in the book. ETFS Battery Tech and Lithium ETF (ACDC) is a fund comprising clean-energy themed stocks – and look at its performance! The aptly ticker-named ETF 'HACK' offers exposure to the cybersecurity megatrend and BetaShares NASDAQ 100 ETF offers exposure to the Nasdaq index (market cap weighted).

The Australian ETF market is considerably smaller than the US ETF market, however, at around AU$100 billion versus the US$5 trillion asset valuation of the US ETF market. Australia's ETF market is growing, but due to the size, the US market will not only offer you a much broader choice but better liquidity.

## Buying US ETFs – the world is your oyster

If you buy directly on the US stock markets, as I indicated earlier, you are taking a currency risk on one hand but also diversifying your exposure. It really is a very personal choice and will depend on your individual circumstances, but, broadly speaking, you will a greater choice of ETFs in America, just because the industry is that much larger. (For more about the mechanics of buying and selling directly on US markets, see Chapter 8.)

As there is just so much to choose from when it comes to the US ETFs, it's better to research the providers. The top 10 providers are listed in Table 4, following.

**TABLE 4: Top 10 ETF providers in the US**

| iShares (BlackRock) | Proshares |
| --- | --- |
| State Street SPDR | ARK Investment Management |
| Invesco | VanEck |
| Vanguard | Direxion |
| First Trust | Wisdom Tree |

Direxion ETF products are probably for more sophisticated investors, as the ETFs offered appeal to those who want more complex ETF products, such as geared ETFs or that seek to offer non-correlated market performance. Global X offers thematic ETFs, Wisdom Tree provides specialised ETFs and ARK Investment specialises in actively managed disruptive innovation.

Not only can you buy into US stock-related ETFs, but you can also go shopping, metaphorically speaking, across the globe to secure exposure to some of the higher growth international stocks and themes. Think emerging markets, China, Europe, the UK and Latin America. KraneShares specialises in China exposed ETFs.

In Table 5, I have put together a summary of sectors, themes and indices and some ETFs that offer exposure to each of them. The list is not exhaustive: it provides examples only.

**TABLE 5:** Summary of ETFs available in the US

| ETF sector/theme/Index | ETF ticker codes |
|---|---|
| S&P 500 | SPY, IVV, RSP, VOO |
| Dow Jones | DIA, DJD |
| Small, mid cap | IWM, IJH, IJR, IWS |
| Cannabis | MG, MSOS, YOLO, MJ, POTX, THCX, CNBS |
| Decarbonisation/Water/Sustainability | TAN, PBW, PIO, ICLN, CNRG, PBW, QCLN, KGRN |
| EVs | LIT, DRIV, CTEC, KARS, HAIL, BATT |
| Genomics/Biotech | XBI, ARKG |
| Cybersecurity | IHAK, CIBR, BUG, WCBR, UCYB |
| Cloud | SKYY, CLOU, WCLD, IVES |
| Innovation/Technology | QQQ, QQQJ, QQQM, ARKK, ARKQ, CTEC, IVDG, IVSG, XLK |
| Work from home | WFH |
| Data | VPN, BLOK, XDAT |

| ETF sector/theme/Index | ETF ticker codes |
| --- | --- |
| Infrastructure | PAVE, IGF, NFRA, EMLP, SRVR |
| Health care | XLV, VHT, IXJ, IYH, IHF, PTH, IDNA |
| S&P 500 Value | SPYV, VTV, IWD, VBR, IVE, IWN |
| Emerging Markets | IEMG, VWO, EEM, XSOE, SPEM |
| ESG | ESG, AVDR, SUSL, IVLC |
| Robotics | ARKQ, BOTZ, ROBO, IRBO, ROBT |
| Aerospace/Defence | ITA, XAR, PPA, DFEN |
| SPACE – Fly me to Mars | ARKQ, ROKT, UFO and watch this space! |
| Gaming | BETZ, ESPO, BJK |
| Streaming | SUBZ |

The website ETF.com provides a thorough and comprehensive overview of US-listed ETF products.

## Structuring a US ETF portfolio

I am now going to throw some ideas out for you to consider when you are planning on structuring a US-listed ETF portfolio. None of these is meant as advice. The ideas are meant to give you a flavour of what's on offer and how you might consider some long-term, growth ETFs.

Let's assume you are positive about the US economy and you want to have an exposure. I suggest you start big and invest in one of the three major indices' ETFs and then diversify into preferred sectors/themes/country weightings.

As the US economy is one of the world's growth engines, I would always start with exposure to the S&P 500 to capture many sectors in the economy and global growth via the tech giants. As mentioned, you need to decide whether you are happy with the concentration risk of the large tech stocks and will buy an index fund or you look for an equal weighted fund.

If the S&P ETF exposure is the backbone of your portfolio, so to speak, you next need to establish what ribs you want to add. You have many options to diversify into different sectors. For example:

- **Infrastructure**: PAVE is designed to hold stocks that will benefit from US infrastructure development.
- **Dividends**: HDV tracks the Morningstar Dividend Yield Focus Index.
- **Technology**: QQQ tracks the Nasdaq index of the top 100 stocks.
- **Clean energy**: TAN is the Invesco fund that tracks the MAC Global Solar Energy Index.
- **The Chinese market**: KWEB is the KraneShares CSI China Internet Fund.
- **Emerging markets**: IEMG is the iShares Core MSCI Emerging Markets ETF.

The point is, you can mix and match as you go and buy an ETF to suit your needs. If you feel as if you have no idea where to start, the iShares 'Choose your investment goal' webpage (ishares.com) provides excellent information and offers a selection of iShares ETF products for your risk profile.

### What's available in Australia

In Australia, BetaShares, iShares and Vanguard are three of the largest and most popular ETF product providers. If you are looking for a summary of ETFs available in Australia, I would suggest you check out marketindex.com.au and bestetfs.com.au.

Whether you are buying ETFs in Australia or in the US, here is a list of handy hints to assist you in your selection:

- **Diversify:** Don't pop all your money in one hot-to-trot theme ETF. No matter how positive you are about a secular theme, external factors like the bond market can create swift and dramatic changes in the flow of funds across asset classes.

- **Look under the bonnet:** Always check what stocks the ETF holds and how big the ETF is relative to the size of the stocks. Too much money trying to buy a concentration of stocks can lead to overbought and expensive values. It's like trying to thread wool through a small needle.

- **Expense ratios:** Obviously, the higher the ratio, the harder it is for the fund to perform for you.

- **Time in the market:** You can buy your ETF holdings over time and always put together a wish list for the ETFs you want to buy and wait for a market pullback.

- **Be mindful of doubling up:** If you buy an S&P 500 ETF and a Nasdaq ETF (such as QQQ, which has a 45% concentration risk on the large tech giants), you are in effect just buying exposure to Apple, Amazon, Microsoft, Tesla, Alphabet (Google) and Facebook, as both ETFs are heavily weighted to the tech giants.

- **Cyclical/value versus growth:** Spend some time establishing what factor stocks you want exposure to and how that correlates to the stage in the economic cycle. Factors include the categories of momentum (think Tesla), value/cyclical (think energy and banks) and quality/defensive (think health care and consumer stocks).

- **Small caps and the Russell 2000:** ETFs for smaller caps or the Russell 2000 index will offer a larger exposure to the real US economy. The tech giants are as much a global barometer as a barometer to US exposure.

- **Hedging your bets:** Being smart doesn't always pay off. More often than not, trying to hedge your portfolios by buying volatility ETFs (the VIXY ETF tracks the VIX index) or bear/short funds ends in tears. Remember the saying: 'Don't fight the Fed!'
- **Leveraged ETFs:** Some ETFs will use derivative structures and debt to increase the performance of the mandate of the ETF. For example, some ETFs will aim to double the movement in the S&P 500 or double the return on a falling market. Leverage adds risk and, unless you really understand the product, I would leave leveraged ETFs well alone.
- **Consider the NAV:** The 'NAV' or net asset value of an ETF is usually offered live when you buy the ETF. Use a limit order to make sure you don't pay too much and can avoid the ETF if it is trading at a premium to the underlying asset value (sum of the stocks included).

## The next big thing – ESG investing

In the second part of this chapter, I want to introduce you to environmental, social, governance (ESG) investing. According to PRI, ESG (responsible) investing is 'a strategy and practice of incorporating environmental, social and governance (ESG) factors in investment decisions and active ownership asset stewardship'.

ESG investing is an expansion or evolution of the better known 'responsible' or 'ethical' investing, where values and moral codes-based criteria were applied to investment decisions on stock selection. Think the move away from investing in tobacco stocks by large investors in the 1990s. The Presbyterian Church and other religious orders subscribe to faith-based investment themes to align the religious beliefs and stewardship of the funds managed with their religious goals.

ESG investing is one of the fastest growing investment paradigms and reflects the move away from 'shareholder supremacy', a term coined by the famed economist Milton Friedman. Friedman's philosophy was that a company's main duty of care was to the shareholders and its responsibility was to maximise company profits and shareholder returns.

A profit-at-any-cost model could arguably be one of the reasons the world is facing such challenging pollution, slavery, poverty and social inequity issues. The rise in strong-man populist leaders is in part attributed to the ongoing economic impacts from the 2008 GFC and the policy responses that have only served to increase the wealth for the asset rich, while wage growth of the average worker has stagnated.

Increasingly, major fund management companies are recognising there are numerous financial risks to the traditional investing paradigm that need to be managed and accounted for by companies and shareholders.

Passive investing in ESG funds grew sharply in 2020, and the value of ESG ETFs more than doubled from US$82 billion in mid-2020 to US$194 billion in January 2021. Some describe the scope for growth as only the start of the S curve.

The passive ESG ETF figure may seem small; however, over US$40 trillion of assets under management have had some form of ESG filters applied to the investment decisions. According to Pensions & Investments, 'active strategies represent the majority of ESG-related assets under management, at 75% in the U.S. and 82% in Europe'.

The 2021 inauguration of President Biden has further underwritten political will to start tackling issues that are aligned with ESG principles, which will no doubt just increase the move to improved corporate responsibility.

## How does ESG investing work?

Investment managers and investors apply ESG filters to the companies they invest in across three categories:

1. **Environment:** This includes water usage, carbon footprints, carbon abatement, recycling, the erosion of natural capital (global ecosystems) and even what is termed the 'circular economy' (where companies track and try to minimise their footprint all the way through the product life cycle). Logitech is a company that is working actively on such a proposition.

2. **Social:** Including the push to have companies become more equitable, with improved working conditions, parental leave benefits, the cessation of slave-like working conditions and wages (think cheap fashion, blood diamonds, money laundering, the cobalt industry and even global shipping). Around 40 million people are estimated to be caught in some form of slavery; 25 million are in Asia and 70% are women. A shocking one out of four children are also thought to be caught in slave-like working conditions.

3. **Governance:** This includes the move towards improved company governance, with greater gender diversity, removal of gender pay-gaps, diversity of boards, more equitable management of renumeration and transparent reporting systems.

There are several ways to screen stocks and compile fund portfolios. Negative screening or exclusion is the original responsible investment strategy. Fund managers sell off or omit companies because their operations and style do not align with ESG filters. For example, large pension funds have been divesting fossil fuel assets and/or tobacco and gaming stocks.

The alternative to negative screening is positive screening. This is where fund managers and investors actively seek out companies that align with ESG principles and work to achieve good metrics across all the ESG criteria.

ESG integration is probably the newest category, where companies are actively trying to reduce their carbon footprint, for example.

## Why the move to ESG investing?

The pressure for companies to embrace ESG factors is multi-directional, from the people and companies who invest in them to increased regulatory demands and scrutiny, and risk management. Politics of course may play a role in some jurisdictions, but for the next two years at least at time of writing, the largest global nations are uniting with President Biden to accelerate and embed the transition across global investment.

### Future generations are demanding change

The changing demographic of investors and managing retirement funds for future generations are having an impact. Younger investors and the millennial workforce are making their mark.

I really believe traditional investors, in general, are completely underestimating the influence of the younger generation. When the legendary Warren Buffett announced the purchase of a US$4 billion stake in oil company Chevron in February 2020, most people blinked and said, 'Well, that's typical Buffett, value investing in a cheap cyclical stock for the reflation trade'.

But not millennial YouTuber and blogger Gali from HyperChange. He felt compelled to call his investing idol Mr Buffett to account for taking a make-money-at-any-cost approach by buying one of the US oil giants. Paraphrasing the 35-minute YouTube piece, Gali said:

'A part of me almost felt like I died today. There's such a disconnect. Are we investing just to make money? Or do we want to invest in the future we believe in and invest in companies that are changing the world and building it into something we want?'

He continued:

'We need our billionaires and investment idols to inspire us to live more sustainably, and invest in the future they believe in. I'm ashamed as a Warren Buffett fan that he/his company Berkshire Hathaway bought Chevron. It shows they put profit over people and the planet. Lame.'

Although not every gen Z or millennial is as outspoken as Gali, he does reflect the shifting sands of a younger generation who perceive the world differently and want different outcomes for their investment savings. I think we all underestimate this demographic and its potential influence on stock-picking at our own risk.

## ESG investing manages risk

On balance, the ESG focus aims to maintain shareholder returns and in fact improve the long-term performance by reducing risks associated with poor ESG application and adverse risk-taking.

For example, you will hear more about climate risk and stranded assets when it comes to investing in infrastructure assets. As the world moves to clean energy generation, a dwindling reliance on fossil fuel energy (oil, gas and coal) supplies ultimately risks the viability of the assets such as coal-fired power plants and oil and gas plant and equipment. Such assets become what the industry refers to as 'stranded' (having no future value).

There are large costs associated with the asset write-downs. During the 2020 pandemic, write-downs in asset values for the oil and gas industries were estimated at US$150 billion. Although this was a result of the collapse in demand for energy products, the impact of the collapse in demand shows just how much the industry has to lose from global decarbonisation.

Global fund managers have a fiduciary responsibility to ensure the invested returns are not impaired by worthless assets in the future.

(Note: as the industry rationalises, the lowest cost producers will, in the short term at least, benefit from rising oil prices as demand rises. However, long term the industry faces major systemic issues.)

Companies that fail to adapt will risk becoming the losers. Investors may quibble about the valuation of Tesla, but for many gen Zs and millennials, Tesla is actively changing their world for good.

The counter-argument may well assert itself if and/or when the pendulum shifts back to value/cyclical investing or the world experiences another recession.

Although evidence shows the ESG factor stocks outperformed the non-ESG stock indexes over calendar 2020, the moral ESG purpose will be tested in instances when pressure on margins and profits grows, such as during economic slowdowns or recessions.

Increasingly, data from ESG indexes support the theory that companies who adapt and embrace ESG factors increase shareholder returns over time. Or, put another way, quality companies usually exhibit strong ESG factors that have improved not only the financial returns for stockholders but are also reflected in the culture, leadership, adaptability and persistence to achieve over time.

Morgan Stanley, through the MSCI ESG indexes (MSCI = Morgan Stanley Capital International), allows investors to track the performance of companies with an ESG rating versus non-ESG-rated companies.

Beware that not all companies will do the right thing. 'Greenwashing' is a term used to describe companies that pretend to be doing the right thing but in fact are talking the talk but not walking the walk.

Shareholder activism may well keep the greenwashers in check but, as usual, when you are investing your savings into ESG funds I would strongly recommend you always check which stocks are part of the ESG ETF.

## ETFs and ESG investing - the choice is yours

Is cuddly capitalism the way of the future? Will ESG investing force more companies use their profits for purpose? Time will tell how companies approach and deal with some of the greatest challenges since the GFC, from climate change impacts, inequality and risks from rising social movements like #MeToo and #BlackLivesMatter.

As much as the naysayers decry 'doing well by doing good' as virtue signalling or cancel culture, the world listens when Larry Fink, CEO of the largest asset manager BlackRock, writes an open letter pronouncing 'sustainability and climate-integrated portfolios can provide better risk-adjusted returns to investors'.

ESG investing is evolving and although there are constantly improving metrics to measure and assess the ESG factors, all of us come with some value judgements around stocks. Gaming may be acceptable in my world but not in your world, for example. Or you may decide that the tech giants are not the exemplars of ESG factors and decide to look elsewhere and focus on decarbonisation or infrastructure funds.

There are many ways to cut the cake, so to speak. Therefore, as usual, it is always important with all financial products such as

ETFs and ESG-focused funds to view what the stockholdings are and whether you are happy to invest in the underlying securities in the ETF wrapper at that point in time.

## Chapter summary

- Don't be lulled into a sense that ETF products are risk free and will not experience volatility. ETFs may be referred to as passive investments, but in reality the ETF is a complex financial product.

- The ETF market will continue to grow with new product offerings and styles of management. The same principles apply when you buy an ETF as when you buy a stock; allocate some time and research what underlying stocks you are actually investing in.

- ESG investing and metrics will continue to grow as more investors, both professional and retail, subscribe to improved socio-economic and environmental outcomes. The changing of the investment guard from baby boomers to millennials and gen Z will reinforce and accelerate the trend.

# 8

# Building a US stock portfolio

Finally, I can hear you exhale, we've arrived at the all-important chapter on recognising the characteristics of winning stocks and building and managing a portfolio.

As you have discovered, changing technology and ever-evolving investment products are facilitating the avenues to diversify your international and US stock market exposure. The three avenues are via ETFs listed in Australia, managed funds in Australia (which I do not touch on), or investing directly into US stock markets.

There are numerous online platforms available to Australian investors; among the zero-cost platforms are IG Share Trading, CMC Markets and Stake. Other platforms include eToro, Saxo Capital markets, CommSec International, Westpac Share Trading, Interactive Broker and nabtrade.

It's a good idea to look at a few or ask your friends what platform works for them and why.

You might want to consider the following:

1.  The cost of the transaction (brokerage fees or zero cost)

2. Whether there are monthly fees in lieu of lower charges

3. How the exchange rates offered are calculated

4. How the pricing data and your portfolios are provided and displayed

5. Ease of use of the platform and the timeliness of the pricing

6. The security of the platform in terms of protecting your money

7. The availability of education and risk management tools

8. The number of stock markets that can be traded

9. The availability of the platform on different devices or apps

10. Reliability and strength of the platform during high volume trading days.

The premise is that investing directly into the US stock markets creates diversity in your share portfolio and offers access to more themes and opportunities than are available in Australia. The choice and size (liquidity) of the stocks in the US are much greater, which is both a blessing and a curse. It's a blessing because it means there's a lot of money to be made; and a curse because there are just so many stocks to choose from that the process can seem overwhelming.

Writing a book on the US stock markets is similar. When I was planning *Shareplicity 2*, I had to ask myself, 'Where do I start and what do I want readers to take away from the book?'

The answer was to start with the macro or big picture and then focus on how investors can capitalise on favourable big picture themes/sectors to make money. But the story doesn't end there. In some respects, it starts here, where we begin to put your new-found knowledge into practice. In this chapter, we're going to look at:

➤ Planning your investment approach and setting some goals

- ► What makes a winning company
- ► The effect of bond yields on share prices
- ► Risk and volatility – and how diversification helps counter both
- ► Possible US portfolio structures.

## Planning and setting goals

To quote Ernest Hemingway, 'the best laid plans of mice and men often go awry'. In other words, we can start with a plan for the future, only to be presented with unforeseen circumstances that disrupt our goals and plans. However, we still need a plan. Racing to open an online account and hopping onto Reddit and Wall Street Bets and starting to trade is usually not the best approach.

No matter what age you are, I firmly believe that trying to trade stock markets is not the winning strategy for real wealth creation. If you are more patient and allocate the bulk of your savings to picking the winners, leaving just a small pot for trading the Reddit momentum crazes, then you will hopefully kill two birds with one stone. It will enable you to have some fun trading, but you won't place your savings in harm's way and risk losing everything.

Investing in stocks and growing wealth is about patience.

A sound strategy is to target most of your savings towards finding and investing in the next trillion-dollar company. Yes, this should be your plan: to own stocks that will become trillion-dollar giants of the US stock market by 2030. We'd also like to find some emerging giants. 2030 may seem a long way off, but in my four decades of investing I have never seen so many risks and opportunities in the investment world. If you can navigate the risk/reward opportunities, I believe you will be able to benefit from generational wealth creation.

Whether you are starting with a small sum of money or a larger amount, you need to set some goals. Depending on your risk profile (which we look at later in the chapter), you can choose a slower, low-maintenance pathway by selecting ETF products and following a set-and-forget investment approach. Or you can be very actively involved and choose only to invest directly in US stocks, which is called 'active stock-picking'.

If you are unsure of or new to the process, then I would plan to start with the ETFs as the backbone or tree trunk, and branch out (excuse the pun) into direct stocks as your knowledge and confidence grows.

Goals are not set-in-stone, never-to-be-changed targets, but pathways to guide you on your investing journey. They are also very personal. Do not be distracted by 'that person' who made enough money from a company such as Tesla or Afterpay to retire. To achieve that outcome, the investor would have taken a lot of risk and no doubt invested large sums at the outset.

A final note on planning is not to underestimate Lady Luck. Sometimes investors are just there at the right place and time to reap the rewards. Equally, even with the best goals and plans in place, stock markets can deliver really bad returns. That's why you need to understand risk (which we discuss later in the chapter).

## Spotting the emerging winners

Before we move on building an actual portfolio, let's dwell on what makes a winning company.

Michael Mauboussin from Morgan Stanley believes 'the holy grail is large markets with attractive economics'. Sounds simple in theory. How does this look in practice?

Over the following pages we'll look at the attributes that contribute to making potential 'holy grail' stocks.

## A large market for the company's goods or services

In an era of great change, the next giants will operate in new, large total addressable markets (TAMs). A TAM is always usually future-based, not in the here and now. Apple is the textbook case. According to Mordor Intelligence, the smart phone market is now valued at US$714 billion and Apple has an 80% market share. Apple did not start out with the mission to become the world's leader in smart phones. The company just continued to breathe momentum into the market with new product improvements and services. The creation and rollout of 5G technology has under-written the next super-cycle of smart phone usage and adoption. Not every company will achieve a market share statistic of 80%, and nor will Apple necessarily maintain that share, but the point is that large markets offer large money-making opportunities.

## Future growth

Morgan Stanley's research into the top 25% performers of the S&P 500 from 1990 to 2009 shows that the highest source of total shareholder return, and the key driver of long-term stock performance, is revenue growth. You want to own stocks that can grow revenue over time, in excess of the cost of capital used to generate the growth. This means a company can borrow or raise funds through new shares (equity) and use the funds to generate higher revenue growth than the cost of the money raised, via debt or equity.

As is usual with finance, the concept sounds easy, but the reality is that very few companies achieve success in this way. As an investor, if you can pick companies that can achieve a good return on capital, it will pay off over the long term.

## ESG factors

The rise in investors looking at environmental, social and governance (ESG) metrics – as discussed in the previous chapter – will increasingly differentiate between the winning and losing stocks. Not only can sentiment impact on companies, changing government regulations and reporting standards also bring challenges and opportunities.

## Gaining market share through competitive advantage

Competitive advantage (referred to as a 'moat' by Warren Buffett) is one of the most important aspects to determining a company's success. Competitive advantages can be having the lowest cost and best service or product, or the best user experience for customers, facilitated by a new technology that changes the way the consumer works. Whatever form the advantage comes in, the fact that competitors cannot provide the same product or service is what enables a company to be more profitable and gain market share. This usually leads to a higher stock price.

Competitive advantage allows giants to hold on to their leading position in large markets without eroding their margins or market share, and emerging leaders in a new market seek to grow and expand their market share (growth) and improve margins.

A way to do this is through vertical integration of existing business models to apply new features or add one that captures greater usage from a customer. Apple has been extremely successful at this, adding software and app services to its hardware business to create new and profitable revenue streams. The smart phone is not just a piece of funky hardware: it's now your digital wallet, your social media, your app platform and so much more.

Arguably, Tesla is aiming to achieve competitive advantage not only by being the best and lowest cost EV manufacturer, but also through vertical integration of its services, including online sales of EVs (removing costly car dealerships), add-on insurance products and the continuing rollout of FSD or full self-driving software (the autonomous driving feature). Some experts believe the company will generate increasingly more earnings from the software services than the hardware (EVs), in much the same way as Apple is doing with the smart phone.

## Customer loyalty, trust and brand

I don't think there is one example in history of a company that was able to create a great, trustworthy brand for consumers which did not evolve into a great investment. Of course, the comment is a generalisation but, in principle, humans love a great brand; they often become sticky and don't want to change. How many smart phones of the same brand have you bought? Do you have a favourite car company? Companies spend billions of dollars building up brand awareness, but the ultimate success is determined by the quality and safety of the service or product and how well it meets the customer's needs. Great brands usually equal great trustworthy products and services. Brand quality and reputation matter.

Piper Sandler's Spring 2021, Taking Stock with Teens® survey reflects just how important strong brands are to a company's success. If you can capture the youth, then there is a good chance they will stick with the brand for life. Would it surprise you to learn that Apple, Nike, Amazon, Starbucks and Netflix all topped the charts for brand loyalty and market share in this segment? I think not, and these are excellent examples of great brands creating great companies and shareholder wealth.

## Creating shareholder value

*'A company's objective should not be simply to grow; it should be to grow such that it creates value. A company creates value when its investments earn a return higher than the opportunity cost of capital.'*

– Morgan Stanley, 'The Math of Value and Growth'

Again, this statement reads as a simple concept but, in reality, more companies fail at achieving this goal than we would like to admit.

To create shareholder value, there are so many moving parts a company and management need to navigate. Corporate culture is important. Does the company have good reporting systems and is the workforce inclusive? How diverse is senior management and the board? Does the CEO have a vision? Can the company create real barriers to entry through having the best product in class?

Some influences are beyond the control of the management and the company. These include a global pandemic or shifts in market and investor sentiment and increases in the cost of capital (as interest rates rise).

However, great management is able to navigate the external impacts, adapt and change when necessary, remain resilient and maintain innovation and technological investment to stay one step ahead of the competition.

## How rising bond yields impact on companies and valuations

Although you learnt earlier that falling interest rates are generally good for stocks and rising interest rates can pose challenges for stock markets, I want to explain in a little more depth the three reasons why this is the case. My aim is to help you understand how the bond (US Treasury) markets can change the course of stock markets. All three principles are derived from mathematical calculations, but for our purposes understanding the concepts is more important.

Rising US bond yields, particularly the 10-year treasury bond yields, have three main impacts:

1. **They alter the opportunity cost of owning stocks:** In the same way as you feel compelled to seek a higher return on

your savings from the stock market when interest rates are low, the inverse happens when treasury bonds (interest rates) rise. The reason is that the investor will seek a higher return to offset the risk of holding the stock versus buying bonds. If you can earn 5% on a bond, then you would expect at least a 10% return on your stocks (5% to match the bond return and at least 5% for the risk of holding the stock).

2.  **The cost of capital impacts on valuations:** Stocks are often valued according to the expected future cash flows (earnings) that are discounted back to a present-day value, to give investors a current-day valuation for the company's future earnings (think five years out). This valuation is used more for growth companies that have what is referred to as a 'long earnings tail' (i.e. profits come in the future).

    Because of inflation, the value of money (cashflow earnings in this instance) needs to be worth more in the future than the present. To gauge what amount future earnings will be in current-day value terms, the forecast must be adjusted by a discount rate (rate of interest) to bring it back to a present-day valuation. If the stock price is lower than the present-day valuation, then the stock appears to be good value. If the discount rate rises, the present-day value falls and vice versa. Put simply, $100 in 10 years' time will have a higher value in the present if the discount rate is lower.

3.  **The cost of borrowing increases:** As the bond yield rises, so can the cost of borrowing. A higher cost of debt makes it more challenging to earn a higher return on the capital invested – that is, the company will need to generate more cash flow to cover the interest payments.

Before you start your portfolio construction, you need to have a long-term view of where you see the world and the US economy heading. Will there be slower GDP growth in future?

Will disruption, innovation and technology continue to play a role in changing business models and the way we work?

Shareplicity sits firmly in the camp that the pandemic has perversely accelerated the world towards further technological innovation. We have come to realise the interconnectedness of humanity with nature, and now appreciate that environmental degradation and destruction of our ecosystems leave not only us but our economies vulnerable to major systemic shocks such as the pandemic.

Ironically, the economic responses (both fiscal and macro-economic policies) have put in train one of the sharpest V-shaped economic recoveries in years.

However, I do not believe the world is heading back to what we knew in terms of GDP growth, driven by demographics (population growth) and consumption. There will be too much disruption with machine learning and robotics, data analytics and everything discussed to date: meaning, the traditional recovery that the world is experiencing will only go so far. The real growth will continue to be generated with a backdrop of an historically lower-for-longer interest rate world.

Of course, your view may be totally in contrast to mine; none of us knows the future.

However, we can risk-adjust our portfolios to enable the powers of compounding to work. We do this by buying into quality stocks in themes and sectors and countries where we believe future growth will flourish.

Just remember, the value of your portfolio will not always go up in a straight line: sometimes the money flows will switch from different sectors and themes in the market. By knowing the stocks you invest in and having a plan, you will hopefully not be drawn into the emotional turmoil that volatility in stock markets can create.

## Understanding risk and volatility

Stock markets can create problems for investors, who may allow their emotions to influence how they manage the risks attached to investing. Most investors struggle with volatility, including yours truly. Volatility is defined in the Shareplicity playbook as how much stock prices fall or appreciate. Some stocks exhibit lower volatility, which for some investors seems boring or too old-fashioned – think the standard family sedan car or the tortoise. Other stocks are racier – think of Tesla as the hare.

However, higher volatility stocks will generally deliver higher investment returns, hence they can be so attractive.

Statistically, volatility represents how much a stock price swings around the mean (average) stock price. The more a stock goes up and down in excess of the market fluctuations, the more volatile the stock is, bringing big highs (rewards) and big lows (sell-offs or drawdowns).

I think you now have the picture. So how can volatility impact on risk?

Volatility simply has the capacity to invoke a greater emotional response from investors.

Volatility engages the most basic emotions of fear and greed for investors: fear when prices fall, because you start to question your strategy and stock choices, and consider panic-selling at what transpires to be the bottom of the market.

On the flipside, investors get greedy when a stock price keeps rising and they think they should buy in or buy more. Sometimes the price is going up due to a case of FOMO rather than because of the stock's fundamentals – there are simply far more buyers than sellers. The stock has captured the imagination of trend/momentum followers.

Can you see where I am going with this discussion? Volatility is always working to undermine our emotions and up-end our strategy.

Although many expert investors and quantitative investors (the number-crunchers) attach numerical statistics to risk, I prefer to classify risk simply as the potential for me to lose money. I don't like losing money, nor do I like being a forced seller in any situation, because that is when mistakes are made. That's why we need to construct a portfolio that balances the risks with the rewards – and to do this it needs to be risk-adjusted.

The risk-adjusted portfolio is a mix of buying stocks that capture the performance of themes, sectors, indices and global markets via ETF products, and then adding actively selected stocks in which you invest directly. The theory is that the direct stockholdings will create real wealth over time.

## Positive and negative volatility

A friend asked me the other day, 'How do you know when to sell?' Knowing when to hit the sell button rather than adding more stock in the sell-off is probably the most challenging aspect of investing.

The answer comes down to knowing your companies; in the absence of something untoward happening to earnings in the future, you should aim to buy more of a stock in the sell-off, depending of course on how much you already own of that stock. This can be referred to as 'positive volatility', meaning the sell-off is a positive opportunity.

On the flipside, negative volatility is when stocks sell-off for a good reason, and this is when you need to understand that the market is offering signals that it is time to sell. Averaging down can sometimes be the worst nightmare for investors, if you do not fully appreciate why the stock is falling.

## Mix and match your way to risk management

'Don't put all your eggs in one basket' might seem like a worn-out trope, but the keys to investing success are managing risk and diversifying your stock portfolio. How you construct your portfolio depends a lot on your age and income streams. For example, as you move to retirement, you generally want less volatility and more security. Conversely, when you are young and have a high earnings capacity, you will most likely embrace more risk, go for the high-flying stocks and possibly place large positions on just a few of them.

The truth is, you are more than welcome to put all your eggs in one basket, so long as you understand how the story may end – there's always the chance you will trip and break all the eggs. In stock market terms, the one big investment might not work out or, worse, it does work out but you panicked and sold when volatility struck.

Equally, I am conscious of understanding and managing my risk by doubling or tripling my exposure through an ETF product and holding a stock directly. For example, if you own Apple, Microsoft, Amazon and Tesla, as I do, then owning the S&P 500 market cap weighted ETF in effect means I have double the exposure. Remember how we looked at the weightings of stocks in ETFs in Chapter 7?

There is nothing wrong with a doubling-up strategy in a market, but remember, when the flow of funds turns you will experience drawdowns (sell-offs in both the ETFs and the stocks).

Here's why a mix and match structure can work for you:

- ► You cannot possibly be an expert on picking all the stocks, particularly in some of the more specialised and technical areas of the market, such as genomics.

- ► You are investing from afar and, even though social media and the internet have provided much better access to information, your geographic location means you just don't have the same perception and understanding of some of the goods and services that are provided through the companies you want to invest in.

- ► It is very tempting to own too many stocks, so manage your portfolio to ensure you are happy with the quality of the stocks you own.

- ► You can diversify between indices, themes and sectors, using a combination of ETFs and stocks.

- ► You can match your portfolio to the great baskets of stocks.

## Baskets of stocks

To help you make your choice of stocks, I have expanded on the three categories discussed in Chapter 4 to give you more granularity and description of the US stocks. This process will hopefully make it easier for you to pick the stocks you want to own in different parts of the economic or interest rate cycles.

The baskets are themed: defensive quality growth, cyclical value, secular growth, cyclical quality growth and asset valuation plays.

Let's run through the baskets and the differing characteristics.

## Defensive quality growth

Companies exposed to businesses that generate recurring income from consumer staples (food, groceries, cleaning, washing products, etc.) and health care companies are generally regarded as having defensive earnings streams. The earnings streams are typically more stable and reliable through the economic cycles, as we all need to buy these goods.

If the company generates strong cash flow and has a strong balance sheet, the stocks are often thought to be good performers during periods of economic slowdown and recessions. Their earnings are influenced more by demographics such as population growth and aging populations. Some of the older biotech companies, for example, have been long-term winners for the aging baby boomer demographic.

These companies are not immune from disruption from ecommerce, ESG impacts (think the carbon footprints and the sourcing of raw materials) and competition (genomics).

The unexpected benefits from a lockdown economy in the year of the pandemic allowed some consumer staple companies to benefit from the boom in cleaning products, such as Clorox.

I want you think about the big names in this basket, such as Coca-Cola, PepsiCo, Procter & Gamble, Walmart, Costco, Merck, Regeneron and AbbVie.

## Cyclical value

Cyclical value stocks are those companies whose products or services are more impacted by the general economic backdrop. They often produce or sell 'consumer discretionary' items such as cars, whitegoods, travel (hotels, airlines, restaurants), clothing and luxury goods. When the times are good (and economic activity is strong and robust), we basically spend more on these non-essential goods and services.

There are many examples in the US stock markets of cyclical value stocks. Think of the big brands such as General Motors, Ford, Boeing, airlines, travel stocks such as Hilton, MGM and Wynn Resorts, Ralph Lauren, Tiffany & Co., Estee Lauder, Bed Bath & Beyond.

Energy companies such as the oil and gas companies are regarded as cyclical value stocks. I suggest you are mindful of the short-term investment versus the longer term investment case for these stocks with the increased push towards decarbonisation.

Companies exposed to mining, infrastructure and development, such as Deere and Caterpillar, fall into this basket too.

Value stocks possess what is referred to as 'operating leverage', meaning that when demand picks up, the revenue drops to the bottom line (earnings) as many of the costs are fixed and fully depreciated.

### Secular growth

Secular growth was discussed in detail over the megatrend chapters, so I am thinking you have the gist now. But no matter how powerful the tailwinds are for secular growth, there are always competitive pressures and macro-economic or cyclical impacts.

### Cyclical quality growth

There is some overlap between secular growth and cyclical quality growth. Even the giants that are exposed to the megatrends will, at some stages in the economic cycle, be impacted. For example, Google has a huge exposure to global advertising spend; Amazon sells discretionary goods online (although the Prime model mitigates the cyclical nature as it is a recurring revenue 'rundle' service); the demand for new iPhones will vary depending upon the stage of the cyclical innovation; and many investors are waiting to see how Tesla will ride out the next economic downturn.

It is worth pausing to note that great cyclical growth companies can navigate and adapt to periods of stress and change. The pandemic has been a test of resilience and flexibility to adapt in extreme conditions. Arguably, the leaders in the finance sector would fall into this category. PayPal and Square, for example, or JPMorgan Chase, Goldman Sachs or Morgan Stanley. I would also put Nike, Google and Microsoft in this category.

## Asset valuation plays

Real estate investment trusts and/or conglomerates (a group of non-correlated businesses within one company such as Wesfarmers in Australia or General Electric) can be considered as asset valuation plays, meaning the sum of the parts exceeds the current value. The divisions are often worth more when sold off rather than sitting in an agglomerated company (parent or holding company).

Concerns over antitrust regulation for the technology giants might be mitigated if breakups occurred to reduce their market power and influence. For example, AWS (the cloud business) for Amazon may be worth more as a stand-alone company than when it is owned under the Amazon umbrella.

Real estate investment trusts should be evaluated carefully, as the ongoing disruption to traditional business models means that, for example, shopping mall owners and operators are set to struggle with the growth in ecommerce. They are also exposed to secular themes, including NextEra Energy, Crown Castle International and Equinix.

## A sweet spot for interest rates

The simple rule of thumb is that the sweet spot for stock investing is when interest rates are between 2 and 3%, such as in the

Goldilocks economy we referred to in Chapter 4. At this level, economic growth is robust but economies are not overheating – which can lead to interest rate increases.

Negative to low interest rates infer poor economic conditions, and when interest rates are too high, stocks generally won't perform. This is because inflation or inflationary expectations will drive investors into more inflation-protected assets such as property and commodities.

The reflation trade, you may recall, is when economic activity is picking up and investors switch their stock portfolios from the more defensive companies and the technology and growth companies to the cyclical and cyclical growth companies.

## US stock market sectors

Table 6 shows a broad summary of the US sectors, the ETF ticker code, what basket they may fit into and how interest-rate-sensitive the stocks are. (The sectors are presented in alphabetical order.) However, as usual, if you decide to stock-pick then you will need to research the companies, as there is a lot more happening than just the basket selection. The baskets provide context and help you understand how the flow of funds will alter and change when sentiment and macro-economic factors alter.

## TABLE 6: US sectors, ETFs, stocks and baskets

| Sector | ETF code | Stock examples | Basket | Interest-rate-sensitive |
|--------|----------|----------------|--------|------------------------|
| Communication Services | XLC | Verizon, Facebook, Comcast, Disney, Netflix, AT&T | Secular growth, cyclical value and cyclical quality growth | This is a classic example of a sector where the basket will vary depending on the stock and shows just how important it is to understand what stocks are included in the ETF or sector. Valuations are likely to be impacted by rising interest rates. |
| Consumer Discretionary | XLY | Carnival, Grubhub, Lululemon Athletica, Amazon, Tesla, Home Depot, McDonald's, Nike, Target | Cyclical quality growth | This sector is very stock specific, but these companies should perform well when economic activity improves. |
| Consumer Staples | XLP | Coca-Cola, Colgate-Palmolive, Procter & Gamble, Walmart, Altria, Philip Morris, Estee Lauder | Defensive quality growth | Valuations impacted by rising interest rates. Perform better when economic outlook is more uncertain. |
| Energy | XLE | Exxon Mobil, Schlumberger, Halliburton, Chevron | Cyclical value | Yes, typically, energy stocks benefit from economic activity. There are threats to long-term demand from decarbonisation. |

| Sector | ETF code | Stock examples | Basket | Interest-rate-sensitive |
|---|---|---|---|---|
| Financials | XLF | Berkshire Hathaway (insurance), JPMorgan, Bank of America, BlackRock, Morgan Stanley, Goldman Sachs | Cyclical value, cyclical quality growth | Financials, particularly the commercial banks, benefit from rising interest rates (as this assists their lending margins). Investment banks – Goldmans and Morgan Stanley and asset manager BlackRock – benefit from strong financial markets. |
| Health Care | XLV | Johnson & Johnson, Pfizer, Abbott Laboratories, Eli Lilly | Defensive growth | Valuations under pressure when interest rates are rising. |
| Industrials | XLI | Honeywell, Boeing, 3M, Caterpillar, General Electric, Deere, Lockheed Martin | Cyclical value, cyclical quality growth | Yes, although 3M was a major beneficiary of the pandemic via the demand for PPE (personal protective equipment). |
| Information Technology | XLK | Apple, Microsoft, Visa, Nvidia, Mastercard, PayPal, Intel, Adobe, Salesforce, Cisco | Cyclical quality growth, secular growth | As the tech giants are in this sector, remember that some have significant secular tailwinds. Rising interest rates and inflationary expectations can put pressure on stock valuations. |

| Sector | ETF code | Stock examples | Basket | Interest-rate-sensitive |
|---|---|---|---|---|
| Materials | XLB | Linde PLC (gas) DuPont de Nemours (chemicals) Newmont (gold) Freeport-McMoRan Dow Inc (chemicals) | Cyclical value | Yes, this sector benefits from reflation trade and expectations of expanding economic growth, also from rising inflationary expectations. |
| Real Estate | VNQ | Crown Castle, American Tower, Equinix, Public Storage, Simon Property Group | Asset valuation, secular themes exposed (5G and data storage) | Very interest-rate-sensitive. Typically, real estate trusts benefit from falling interest rates, as the cost of capital decreases the values rise – as do the attractive aspects of the yield for investors. |
| Utilities | XLU | NextEra Energy, Duke Energy, American Water Works, American Electric Power | Defensive growth, asset valuation | Interest-rate-sensitive as investors usually buy for an income stream. Risks associated with ESG metrics, particularly climate change and decarbonisation. |

Source: CNBC

Warren Buffett famously said (and I paraphrase), 'All you need to do is buy stocks that offer you exposure to the great US GDP growth'. But the investing world may have changed irrevocably since the 2008 GFC. The once stable and reliable stocks of the household-name companies that we all know have been left in the wake of the technology giants.

Many investors believe the consequences of monetary and fiscal stimulus will create the strongest US GDP growth in decades, as the economy rises like phoenix from the ashes. This, of course, will bring back into focus the many quality cyclical and cyclical value plays.

How does this narrative align for you when you are constructing and building a US stock portfolio?

Since the beginning of this century, there have been three major sell-offs in the S&P 500:

- the dotcom – a fall of 50%,
- the 2008 GFC – a fall of 57%
- the coronavirus crash of 2020 — a fall of 34%.

But looking back in time since 1950, the three longest periods when the stock market went without a double-digit correction were between 1990 and 1997 (+302%), 2002 and 2007 (+147%) and from late 2011 through to late 2015 (+112%).

The data, as provided by A Wealth of Common Sense, shows that bear markets are less frequent when double-digit corrections occur.

The bottom line for investors is that trying to pick the timing in the market is too hard. Sometimes you'll be too early and other times too late. If you can aim to ride out the drawdowns and even invest more during the pullbacks, then history shows there are eye-watering gains to be made.

## Example portfolio for 2021

Following is an example of how I would structure a US stock portfolio in 2021. Please remember this is not advice – you need to make your own decisions, based on your own circumstances and risk profile.

I would apply the mix and match approach via ETFs and direct stock investments.

The portfolio is designed to go through the cycle and will thus hold some investments that will not perform so well – the utilities and REITs – if expectations of inflation rise. However, the reason for exposure to these stocks is the underlying secular themes.

Quality remains important and will feature across some of the stocks selected (although I know many investors do not consider Tesla a quality stock).

Creating your US/global stock portfolio can be achieved in various ways and each will require varying levels of input. The low-maintenance portfolio is a more set-and-forget approach, where savings can be invested over time.

As you move to the medium-to-high-maintenance portfolio suggestions, more stocks are added, and the numbers of ETF products reduced. These portfolios will require more time, research and effort to manage. That is not to infer you trade daily or even weekly: rather, you may want to revisit the stocks quarterly and add to some or remove/sell down others.

The essential takeaway is that the more you concentrate your portfolio into fewer stocks or ETFs, the more each holding will impact on the performance of the portfolio (in both a positive and negative manner).

**TABLE 7: Portfolio suggestions**

| Low maintenance | Medium maintenance | High maintenance |
|---|---|---|
| 100% ETFs – 10 ETFs at 10% weighting each | 50% ETFs – 5 ETFs at 10% weighting each<br><br>50% stocks – 10 stocks at 5% weighting each | 20% ETFs – 4 ETFs at 5% each<br><br>80% stocks – the more stocks, the less risk per stock<br><br>Less risk: 16 stocks at 5% each<br><br>More risk: 8 stocks at 10% each |

Some of the indices and themed ETFs, as well as stocks you could consider for a portfolio, are listed below. Remember, some will move in and out of favour depending upon the macroeconomic picture:

1. **Exposure to the S&P 500.** This is always a good place to start for exposure to the US economy and the global giants. You have either a market cap or equal weighted option; the former is better when you want more exposure to the large global technology stocks.

2. **Russell 2000 ETF.** For exposure to the smaller companies, which should benefit from the fiscal stimulus and the reopening of trade (as vaccines are rolled out). Think of this as the heart and the soul of the US economy.

3. **China ETF.** Long-term secular growth story.

4. **Emerging markets ETF.** This is an alternative to the China ETF for favourable long-term demographics and will benefit from a weaker US dollar and global economic expansion.

5. **Clean energy ETF.** Secular theme; or an EV, solar or ESG ETF.

6. **Cybersecurity, space, genomics ETFs.** If you're looking to add some 'wow' to the portfolio, then the riskier ETFs will offer you just that!

7. **Conservative stock selection.** Selective banks such as JPMorgan, Morgan Stanley or Wells Fargo for a turnaround; Honeywell and Dupont as industrial cyclical value stocks; Caterpillar and Deere for exposure to infrastructure and commodities; stalwarts such as Disney, Nike and Starbucks; MGM, Penn Gaming and/ or DraftKings® for gaming exposure and reopening trade; disruption and innovation stocks with secular themes such as Square, PayPal, Tesla, Nvidia, Zillow, Apple, Amazon, Microsoft, Shopify, Roku, Teledoc; software services such as Salesforce, Atlassian, CrowdStrike; NextEra Energy for clean energy; Equinix (data centres); Crown Castle for 5G infrastructure; DR Horton, Lennar or Toll Brothers for exposure to the house-building sector; Boeing, Northrop Grumman or Lockheed Martin for aerospace and defence.

## Chapter summary

- ► The macro-economic backdrop can change through the cycles, so diversification is key between ETFs and stocks.

- ► Look for stocks that can create shareholder value by growing their revenue and earnings at rates in excess of the cost of capital and through the economic cycles.

- ► Identify stocks that can function profitably in large TAMs with a robust brand and strong customer loyalty.

- ► Remember, movements up and down in the US 10-year treasury will impact on stock valuations and how the flow of funds moves through the stock market.

- ► Know your stocks, understand your ETFs.

# Extending your knowledge and understanding of the markets

As the sun sets on *Shareplicity 2*, I want to spend some time discussing three interesting topics, that each in their own way can have an impact on your investing experience and the decisions you make.

The first topic focuses on an excellent research paper, 'Liquidity Cascades', which shares some interesting thoughts on how the policies of the Federal Reserve have collided with two other narratives to create a self-enforcing loop of market behaviour.

The second topic often poses challenges for investors: namely, differing valuation calculations and when they are most appropriate for sectors and stocks.

The third topic is knowing when to sell, as breaking up is so hard to do!

## Liquidity Cascades

There is no better quote to describe where the world is heading than paraphrasing Cathie Wood's 'better, cheaper, faster, more productive and more creative', as the influences of the techno-logical disruptive forces of innovation play out on businesses, markets and industries.

The world of investing is no more immune from technological, disruptive innovation. But what happens when a number of factors and narratives come together and create some overarching distortions or risks to financial markets?

Although we learnt about some of these in Chapter 3, when we reviewed how the big picture or the macro-economic back-drop has shaped investing, I now want to go one step further to appreciate how markets, to some degree, are guided by forces that transcend any historical context.

What do I mean?

In 2020, Corey Hoffstein from Newfound Research published an excellent paper called 'Liquidity Cascades'. The paper explored how three major narratives have evolved in stock and financial markets and these trends in turn could be creating more volatility in stock markets and greater drawdowns in the sell-off events.

## The moneyness of markets

As noted in Chapter 8, three major drawdowns have occurred since the turn of the century and each time the central banks – specifically, the Federal Reserve – came to the aid of the stock markets and, more recently, the debt markets.

The paper explores how the Federal Reserve's responses have expanded with each market collapse as they played an ever-greater role in resuscitating the system.

In the 1990s, under Federal Reserve chairman Alan Greenspan, the Fed's response was confined to lowering interest rates. By the 2008–09 GFC, chair Ben Bernanke used QE to buy up assets that institutions could no longer support, such as the mortgage-backed securities.

By the 2020 coronavirus crash, the Federal Reserve was buying junk bonds as the corporate high yield market had (for lack of a better word) stopped working. They have continued this response by rolling out the most significant bond-buying programme to date.

Mr Hoffstein rightly points to the 'moneyness' of the markets. The Federal Reserve has, in simple terms, been responding by adding money to the financial systems and the correlation between global financial assets has become more intertwined. As noted in Chapter 3, the central bank is now an active and, on certain occasions, the main player in financial markets.

If the statement 'too big to fail' ever had credence, then I think you can assume the world's financial markets have definitively moved to that level of significance.

The way in which our financial wellbeing is now completely interconnected and inextricably linked through our savings, pensions, superannuation and other financial assets – such as property – means that the functionality of global financial markets needs to be sustained, to ensure the system won't break down.

When my partner and I recently took out a mortgage with Liberty Financial (the first for me in decades), it occurred to me that I could effectively buy exposure to our mortgage by purchasing Liberty Financial shares on the Australian stock market. I could further increase my exposure by investing in the resulting mortgage-backed security that would be bundled up with other mortgages and issued in the form of a corporate bond.

This is a very simplistic example, but I think it depicts how the tentacles of even a simple loan create interconnectedness between financial assets – and, for that matter, other asset classes such as property and, more recently, the often-debated cryptocurrencies.

How much the valuations of these assets have been inflated by low interest rates, and whether financial assets are now in historical bubble-like territory, really comes down to context and opinions, as values move up and down over the cycles. But, the thing about bubbles is we don't know we are in one until the bubble bursts.

Paraphrasing former Australian Securities and Investments Commission (ASIC) Chairman Greg Medcraft, 'when bubbles burst markets recover, humans don't, so stay very diversified'.

Of course, the talk of bubbles and the moneyness of markets sounds scary, but the prospect of going out of the system is by definition either not possible or desirable for most people. Arguably, some people hedge against the system via alternative assets such as gold; however, for this book at least, the discussion is around stocks.

To sum up the first narrative, the system has evolved to the stage where the financialisation of the world is not going away anytime soon.

### The rising flow of money into passive funds

The second narrative from Mr Hoffman's paper explores the growth in passive investing via ETF products, or the fund management systems that follow an index in an actively managed fund, such as a US mutual (pension) fund. The term 'closet index huggers' is often used to describe this type of investing behaviour.

The increase in 'passive' investing is having a large and material impact on what stocks are being drawn in and out of favour with absolutely no correlation to value or pricing. According to Morningstar statistics, over 50% of all equities owned in the US are in passively managed funds (these can be both ETF wrappers or mutual funds that track the index).

This means for every $1 that is invested in an index market-cap-weighted tracker, a basket of underlying stocks is bought. Equally, the more the funds flow from saving accounts into passive funds, the more underlying baskets of stocks the managers must buy.

Do you ever consider when you buy an ETF, for example, how expensive the underlying Apple or Microsoft stock is versus JPMorgan or Tesla?

Not all stocks are valued the same way or ascribed the same valuation. When you buy an index, it is like buying a mix of fruit and vegetables with no thought given to which produce is cheap because it's in season and which is chronically expensive because it is out of season or has travelled miles from its place of origin.

Similarly, technology and innovation now allow us to partake in some of the stock investing pie without too much thought about those tedious fundamentals that so many of us have read and reread about!

Can you see how purely the weight of money or liquidity (as outlined in Chapter 3) can drive savings out of bank accounts and into ETF or passive funds, because investors have been promised great long-term returns?

The theory is correct, but do not underestimate the potential impact on funds' flows when valuations and reality around the underlying stocks are removed in favour of trends and themes.

Mr Hoffstein highlights that the same happens to the active manager who realises that they now have to sell a certain factor, for example growth, because inflation is expected to rise. If the flow of funds all move from one direction to another, the moves by definition are exaggerated on both the sell and the buy side.

Again, the moneyness of the market and the flow of funds allow for valuations to become stretched at both ends of the rubber band: meaning momentum (trend following) has become very pronounced and has the potential to exacerbate stock price moves to both the downside and the upside. For you, this type of volatility can offer stock-picking opportunities.

## Leverage and complex financial products

The third narrative from Mr Hoffstein's paper is for most of us more challenging to understand. The Federal Reserve's monetary policy responses have distorted financial markets by dropping interest rates to such low levels. You all can appreciate that lower rates mean investors will seek greater returns from other assets other than traditional government-issued treasury bonds, for example, or cash.

The paper puts forward the proposition that the combination of more complex financial instruments and products with associated levels of margin and debt (leverage) and hedging is causing stock markets to become increasingly less liquid. This means they are more fragile at the time of a sell-off event, such as the March 2020 corona crash.

> *'Regardless of whether by design or constraint, a consistent feature of modern markets is rapidly declining liquidity depth during periods of market stress.'*

– Corey Hoffstein, Newfound Research

In a lower-for-longer interest rate environment, financial institutions – such as pension funds and insurance companies with endowment policies – have been forced to move up the risk curve to generate the return needed to meet their fixed future liabilities. In layman's speak, they have needed to develop more complex financial instruments to generate higher returns, as well as pushing more money into equities (with the potential for higher returns).

Financial markets have responded to the Fed's policies by producing a combination of increased options trading, hedging and structured products and high frequency trading (HFT). Options trading has grown in popularity and volume over the last decade. Options are financial instruments giving you the option (with a small amount of money) to buy or sell a stock in the future. Most option trades are facilitated by dealers who, when they offer you the options, must hedge the position in the exact opposite way to create a net square position (meaning they are not winning or losing by allowing you to trade the option).

High frequency traders employ computers to trade large amounts of stocks over the course of a day. Typically, the HFT will use margin (debt) to facilitate the trades. You may have seen the impact of an HFT that goes awry in what is referred to as a 'flash crash', when a trader with a 'fat finger' inputs the wrong price and a stock can suddenly collapse.

The growth in structured products facilitated by banks offering higher returns to investors by selling volatility options to create yield, and leveraged or inverse index ETFs such as the bear ETF, also raise the levels of leverage in the markets.

In theory, HFTs are meant to provide liquidity and options are meant to create strategies for investors to either gear their positions into stocks (increase the upside with less initial outlay) or protect the downside if markets fall, known as hedging. In reality, the opposite has occurred: lower to negative interest rates have incentivised greater risk-taking and complex financial products act in concert to reduce, not improve stock market liquidity.

The GameStop fiasco in January 2021 and the spectacular March 2021 meltdown of Bill Hwang's home office Archegos Capital Management, due to stock bets that went awry with large sums of leverage, has caused more than a few headaches for major banks Credit Suisse (booking a US$4.7 billion loss) and Nomura (a US$2 billion loss). Both are sad *histoires* and future textbook examples of how systems may require some regulation and can break down quickly if there is too much debt, not enough transparency and too few participants in receipt of enough knowledge to understand the risks they are taking.

With increased leverage (margin, debt and options) in the system comes problems for liquidity when everyone is rushing to make the same trade.

In stock markets, the unwinding of leverage translates into 'if I can't sell A, I will dump B to raise the money I need'. Then the more the selling gains traction, the more the positions need to be covered, and the more cash needs to be raised. Selling begets more selling.

Experts estimate that over 10 million new traders entered the US stock market in 2020, and many of these new traders have embraced options, fractionated shares (where you can buy a small percentage of a stock) via different platforms and ETF-themed passive products.

Arguably, many of the newer traders are younger generation, and they have no interest in adopting the style of investing advocated by their parents, grandparents or Warren Buffett. They use social media to create positive reinforcement echo chambers, and millions of investors can all make similar trading bets that create pockets of extreme price movements (such as happened with GameStop).

In summary, Corey Hoffstein arrives at a similar conclusion. The extreme interventions of the Federal Reserve have created the 'market incentive loop'.

I would only add that new, low-cost, trading platforms such as Robinhood, and the explosion of new traders in 2020, have created more pockets of extreme market behaviour.

For those of you who are interested in more examples and explanations in complexity and detail, I would highly recommend

Mr Hoffstein's paper. Or you can watch any of the numerous YouTube videos or podcasts on 'Liquidity Cascades: The coordinated risk of uncoordinated market participants'.

The bottom line for you is to stay diversified and recognise that the financial and stock markets are both penalised and incentivised by the Federal Reserve. And the incentives to rectify the system during extreme periods of stress and volatility (sell-offs) make the markets more moneyed and intertwined.

## Valuation metrics explained

Having just explained that stock markets are influenced by the three narratives explored above, you might be wondering why valuations and different calculations of value matter?

The answer is simple: if you understand the reason for major drawdown (market meltdowns) and melt-ups in stocks that move beyond a company's fundamentals, then the extreme price moves or volatility can create investing opportunities for you.

Although some of you may want to undertake your own value calculations, for the most part, valuation calculations are available online and are regularly analysed by the experts. Also, it's not enough to view valuation calculations in isolation (as we touched on in Chapter 8). Value is ultimately what price someone is prepared to pay at the moment of transaction, but without context the price is just a point in history.

You should be aiming to buy great stocks during opportunistic selldowns that will generate stockholder wealth by creating more value – not just in three to six months, but over longer time frames.

Value is a not a static or binary proposition. It has many inputs and variables. For the large part, calculating future valuations is both an art and a science. It's a science because the numbers you input are real and an art because assumptions are always part of any future value calculations.

The following descriptions are not intended as the go-to summary of how to calculate the valuation metrics. The explanations are purely descriptive, not prescriptive, and are intended as an overview to provide some context for you when you are researching stocks.

## Typical valuations used and how you should interpret them

### *Price-to-earnings ratio*

A price-to-earnings ratio (PER) is one of the most commonly used metrics. It is calculated to establish the value of stock based on how many future years of earnings you are buying at the present time.

If the stock price is $100 and the earnings per stock is $10 for the future 12-month period, then the PER is 10x ($100 divided by $10). It would take you 10 years of earnings to cover the cost of your investment.

If the company makes $2 more than the forecast, or $12 earnings per share, assuming the multiple stays at 10x, on next year's earnings the stock price would rise 20%.

Stock prices will rise because the earnings per share are rising more than forecast. If the company can produce higher than historical earnings in the future, this will most likely lead to what is called 'PER expansion' – the term used to describe a higher PER multiple.

A stock's PER can be compared to both the industry sector and the overall stock market PER.

If you were to work backwards to understand the stock price target in 12 months' time, you would say you expect the stock to generate earnings per share of $10 and it typically trades around a 10x the sector PER multiple: therefore the fair value for the stock is $100.

If the stock price is lower than $100, then some investors would argue the stock is cheap or undervalued. If the stock is more than $100, then the company might be considered overvalued in the short term.

Historically, the S&P 500 has traded as low as 5x future earnings when interest rates were at their peak in 1981, and as high as 25x when interest rates have been at record lows.

### *Dividend yield*

The dividend yield is the amount paid to stockholders, normally quarterly in the US, divided by the stock price. Dividends are usually paid when a company has generated excess cash and it wants to reward stockholders with income.

High dividend yields are often termed 'value traps'. The yield is too good to be true, meaning the company cannot sustain the size of the payments relative to the earnings per share.

Stock market strategists often compare the yield on the stock market to the yield on the US 10-year treasury bond to gauge whether the risk/reward is appropriately matched between stocks versus bonds. If the yield on the stock market or stocks is higher than bonds, then the risk/reward is positive towards stocks.

### *Enterprise value*

Enterprise value (EV) was developed to provide a more efficient metric to value companies. It takes into account the stock price and its level of net debt. Enterprise value is the total market cap (stock on issue multiplied by the stock price) less net debt (total debt less cash on hand).

Enterprise value-to-sales or revenue is used to determine a value (net of debt) for how much sales the company is generating (see below).

Enterprise value to EBITDA (earnings before interest, tax and depreciation or amortisation or cash flow) is a valuation used to see how much the company's value is relative to the cashflow earnings it produces.

Enterprise value is a very useful metric, as just looking at the earnings via a PER of a company does not shed any light on how much debt the company has employed to create those earnings. Nor does a PER shed any light on how the growth and value is being created. In fact, traditional valuations often distort the answers in favour of traditional cyclical, capital-intensive businesses.

Or do they? The lines between different valuation metrics go to the heart of some of the traditional schools of thought. Cutting to the chase, the value of capital-light businesses or weightless companies like SaaS businesses, versus traditional manufacturing companies, essentially lies in where the earnings and costs are being generated.

Both business models generate revenue, however technology or software companies often have much higher variable costs to create the revenue due to higher employee costs, cloud hosting costs such as AWS or Azure, and the cost of leasing premises.

Asset-rich companies have steady operating costs (wages) to generate the revenues and have much higher earnings before interest, tax and depreciation, just because of the way the income and costs are accounted for and the structure of the business. Once the fixed costs are made in plant and equipment (and they have been fully depreciated or amortised), then, as the revenue rises, profits will rise correspondingly as the costs of generating the revenue are relatively fixed and accounted for.

For example, if a company makes $100 million in revenue at the bottom of the economic cycle and $5 million in net profit, the net profit margin is 5%. If demand picks up with economic activity and the company makes $120 million in revenue, the profit will rise to $6 million, a 20% increase (assuming costs and margins stay the same); i.e. the company has not reached peak capacity.

A SaaS company, by comparison, will need in some instances to hire more people to generate 20% sales revenue growth, until the business model becomes more sustainable (i.e. reliable) and the customers have moved by way of example to a subscription service.

The assets of tech companies are its employees. Usually, the more customers you want, the more employees and support services you need, particularly in the early growth stages of the business. This means SaaS businesses often spend a lot more on variable costs such as employees (coders for example) to generate revenue growth, such that earnings can be compressed at the EBITDA level of the profit and loss statement.

The sweet spot for software companies is to be able to create what is referred to as 'scalable' growth, meaning the business continues to grow but the incremental costs for each new customer go down.

### Enterprise value (EV) to sales or revenue

To calculate this metric, you divide EV by sales (revenue) generated. As the net debt has been subtracted, the valuation offers a better appreciation of how much capital is needed to grow revenues.

High-growth companies are often valued on EV-to-sales and the metric can often be high in expectation that there will be considerable future revenue growth. Valuations, of course, will drop steeply if the expected revenue is not forthcoming.

EV-to-EBITDA or cash flow is a traditional valuation method used to assess how expensive or cheap a business is, after the debt is accounted for, to create cash flow.

### Rule of 40

The growth in software and SaaS business models has resulted in a new 'rule of thumb' measurement used by the private equity and venture capitalists, and some investors also use it to measure the performance of these companies, which generally don't report profits.

The Rule of 40 provides an indication of the trade-off between growth and earnings.

Rule of 40 is equal to the sum of revenue growth or decline from one period to the next added to the EBITDA margin (usually) for the same period. If the sum is 40 or greater, then the company has created an appropriate mix between generating revenue growth and managing costs.

Most expert analysts look to metrics like the Rule of 40 and the revenue retention and customer retention of the business.

To take an example, if we look at recently listed SaaS company Datadog, in 2020 it generated 66% sales revenue growth and had a negative EBIT margin (−2.3%). The sum gives you 63.7 (66 less 2.3). Although this is a high result, over time investors will be looking to see that a company like Datadog can become more profitable.

### Price-to-discounted cash flow

None of the ratios we're discussing here is necessarily easy to understand and a price-to-discounted cash flow is one of the more complex. Here's how Investopedia defines discounted cash flow:

> 'Discounted cash flow (DCF) is a valuation method used to estimate the value of an investment based on its future cash

flows. DCF analysis attempts to figure out the value of an investment today, based on projections of how much money it will generate in the future.'

You probably recall how compounding works. The value of your investment will double every seven years if the company returns 10% each year. This means you are expecting a higher return on your money invested in the future, otherwise you wouldn't risk losing the money. You also understand that one dollar should be worth more now, in the present, than the future because of inflation.

By reversing this concept, analysts calculate how much cash flow a business will generate in the future to arrive at a current value. The future cash flows and/or profits are estimated and discounted back to a present-day value using the discount rate or the opportunity cost of capital (usually the US 10-year treasury bond). The higher the discount rate, the less the future cash flow is worth in the present day.

A simple way to understand the concept is if someone were to offer you $1500 in three years' time, how much would you be prepared to give them in the here and now for that return in three years?

The current value you are prepared to give will depend on what return you anticipate. For example, if you knew that a 14.5% return was feasible then you would be happy to give $1000 ($1000 compounded at 14.5% per annum equals $1500 in three years – the maths calculation is $1000 × (1 + 0.145) × (1 + 0.145) × (1 + 0.145) = 1500.

If the return were lower, say 7.7%, then you would give $1200 in the present – the maths is 1200 = 1500 divided by 1.077 to the power of 3 or 1.077 × 1.077 × 1.077.

Are you starting to see how the maths works? The present value of a future value will depend on the discount rate (interest rate) and, for company forecasts, the earnings assumptions (sales revenue growth, cost changes, etc.) you make in the future. The discount rate will vary depending upon how risky the company is perceived to be and the cost of finance (interest rate), for example.

Ultimately, you do not want to pay more in the present than you expect will be generated by the company in the future.

Analysts generate a future value of a company through expected future cash flows and profits likely to be generated. They then apply a price-to-earnings ratio to that number, calculate a price target in, let's say, five years (according to the model), then discount that price back, and that gives you the discounted price target (which changes with interest rate levels) to a present-day price.

If the current stock price is below the present-day price as calculated, then clearly buying the stock (based on the future cash flow and profit expectations) is worth taking the risk for.

The problem with such a model is there are so many variables, from the growth rate in cash flows (and the associated assumptions made) to the discount rate; and, if history has taught you anything, forecasting is notoriously challenging. Often, analysts model a variety of assumptions to offer you three possible outcomes that mirror a likely (realistic) case, a conservative or bearish case and an optimistic (bullish) case. It is then up to the investor to determine what level of risk they want to adopt in either buying or not buying the stock.

### Price-to-book value

A price-to-book value or net tangible assets is a metric normally used for financial companies such as banks and insurance companies, property companies, home builders and investment trusts or a conglomerate (diversified) company.

The price of the company is valued against all the assets less the liabilities. If you were to buy the company, you would want to pay less than the book value so that if all the assets were sold off you would still make money.

Assets on a company's balance sheet include property, land, buildings, equipment, even loan books from banks.

## Don't become bogged down in valuation analysis

The key takeaway is that all valuation metrics need to be viewed in the context of the industry sector in which the company operates, the interest rate expectations (as discussed in Chapter 8), the stage of development of company on the S curve (see Chapter 5) and, ultimately, what expectations there are for surprises on the upside or downside (better or worse than expected results). Risk considerations need to be weighed up also, such as whether the business model can produce scalable growth.

Personally, I think too many people become bogged down in the numbers and spreadsheet analysis. That is not to say you shouldn't do the calculations (should you want to), as numerical valuations provide boundaries when stock prices look overvalued. Clearly, some cyclical value-based businesses became too cheap during 2020 at the height of the pandemic, while some of the recent software IPOs have come to the market at eye-wateringly high valuations.

However, just looking at the numbers narrows complex ecosystems down to sets of figures. Great companies have so many more qualitative features beyond just the profit and loss statement and a balance sheet, such as brand and customer love. It is those qualities that deliver the great numbers and tremendous stockholder wealth over the years.

Looking at a one-year static PER will not tell you about the next high-growth giant, nor will it account for investment required to create that wealth and value.

## Why does selling seem to be the hardest word?

Even though we are more than happy to buy a hot tip from a social media page or at a friend's barbeque, we're usually reluctant to sell the hot tip when the stock price has fallen 35% or tripled in value.

If a stock is a great buy at $100 and falls to $80, then surely the stock is a better buy at $80 rather than $100? Or is it?

If a stock has tripled in price, wouldn't you want to take your spoils and celebrate?

I know from painful personal experience that selling at a loss or at a profit always looks easy in hindsight, but the reality is that it can be an emotionally fraught exercise.

What if the stock price goes higher? Or what if the loss-making hot tip eventually comes good? Hope springs eternal for that breakeven price point. There are so many questions and so few actual answers, as every investor is different and every company will have its day in the sun.

Next, consider how you will react when you have made so much money by accident – when the hot tip actually paid off.

When I'm asked, 'How do you know when to sell?', I usually respond with an unsatisfactory 'It depends'.

Yes, I know that is completely NOT the answer you wanted – and that is why so many traders or momentum players have a fixed percentage sell-off point at which to push the sell button. These are referred to as 'stop losses' and they can be triggered at any percentage fall – 10%, 15% or 20%. My hunch is, the more the stock price falls, the less likely you are to want to sell the loser, even when that is exactly what you should be doing.

No one ever knows for certain when the right time is to sell, but there are some guidelines that can help you decipher which is the I-just-got-lucky stock and what are the real winners and losers. Here's my list of these guidelines:

- **Nothing is certain in investing.** Remember Professor Bessembinder's research? Only a few companies will give you great wealth-creating outperformance. But some stocks are always a better bet (investment) than others.

- **Know your stocks.** Even if you have a mix-and-match portfolio of ETFs and direct stock ownership, you really should spend time becoming acquainted with your top picks. How can you get to know your stocks? To save you from trawling through annual reports and company announcements, I'm giving you below a list of my go-to sources of information on US stocks. This list is by no means exhaustive. I'm afraid, in our internet world, one of the greatest challenges is deciding where to source information from. As always, I remain an advocate for quality and understanding the reasoning behind the source taking the position or the opinion they hold. So, here's the list:

  - **CNBC.** There is free information and CNBC Pro is behind the paywall that I subscribe to, which offers more in-depth interviews and up-to-date broker recommendations. The site also provides an excellent summary of all stocks, their earnings, a summary of broker recommendations and historical price charts.
  - **Jim Cramer's The Street.** This is also a subscriber service. It provides excellent fundamental analysis of the go-to list of stocks that The Street refers to as the Bull Pen.

There is also an actively managed stock portfolio for the Cramer Charitable Foundation. Subscribers are informed daily in live time (if you are awake) of the stock changes in the portfolio. There is also a daily rundown and monthly call from Jim Cramer. Like him or love him, I believe he really knows his stuff and is trying to help people make money (and this is a personal view not a sponsored message!).

- **24/7 Waitlist.** This is a free website that offers daily broker recommendations and changes to recommendations, as well as more in-depth coverage of stocks.

- **Twitter.** The times are changing when you can source excellent stock research on your Twitter feed! For newer and less experienced investors, I would tread carefully when using such a platform until you have developed a handle on who really has experience and is well informed. Also, you will need to learn how to differentiate between the momentum players, traders and value or growth investors to see where you fit in the scheme of investing.

- **YouTube.** This is also an information platform for some investors. It is not a regular go-to source for me, but I do like Tesla Daily presenter and longstanding Tesla follower Rob Maurer, who is one of a few (for want of a better expression) 'Tesla aficionados' and analysts.

- **Yahoo and Google Finance.** I don't generally use either, but I have included them for completeness.

- **Fund managers.** I like to hear the interesting views of Gene Munster from Loup Ventures, Ross Gerber at Gerber Kawasaki, Gary Black, Lyn Alden and Beth

Kindig, who is a technology analyst and investor. Most fund managers have a broad social media presence where you can access their views. I follow all of the above mentioned on Twitter, but there are many others with valuable analysis available.

- **Balance the impacts of demand and supply for stocks versus valuations.** The reason I wanted to discuss the 'Liquidity Cascades' narratives was to offer some thoughts by experts around how the demand and supply of stocks can at times outweigh the fundamentals of stock analysis and valuation. By this I mean the ever-increasing disruption that ETF wrapper products may in fact be having on stock prices that you are not aware of. Equally, the leverage in the financial system can create increased volatility and selldowns in stock markets. Being mindful of these factors can assist you in realising that a stock price move is not always a reason for you to change your view. Too many investors become confused or caught out thinking the stock price represents the true value of a stock.

- **Take some profit off the top.** Just remember, you don't have to sell your entire stockholding if you have made a lot of money. You can always just sell a portion to lock in a profit and wait for the opportunity to buy more.

- **Don't wait for a stock price to go higher.** Most companies don't make great investment stocks, so there is an opportunity cost to not selling. For example, even the smallest holdings can be sold and reinvested into a winning stock and the losses incurred will be offset with the gains over time from the winners.

- **Repeated downgrades in earnings are a red flag.** This is what makes the stock a definite sell. One downgrade can happen, two downgrades in a pandemic are allowable, but three downgrades when competitors are doing well suggests there is a structural problem with the business.

- **Beware of disruption.** Remember that many business models potentially face significant and costly technological disruption. Businesses that fail to invest for the future may receive investor interest during cyclical uptrends, but long-term structural challenges lie ahead. If you are lucky, and one of your dogs (poor performers) is rewarded, then you will have the opportunity to sell and buy into a potentially winning stock.

- **Differentiate between a bubble and a winner.** As highlighted in our discussions about new megatrends, a large TAM will attract many entrants, not all companies will survive and not all will become winners.

## Chapter summary

- Stock markets are ever-changing and evolving. Keeping an eye on the big picture of what influences are moving markets should help you differentiate between the bubbles and the speculative stocks versus the great buying opportunities.

- Diversify, diversify, diversify – particularly if you have a low risk tolerance.

- Valuation metrics will vary depending on the industry sector and stage of business development. Don't become too obsessed by the numbers or you will miss the great quality companies.

- Selling is an important feature of investing and, while selling is not always easy, there is nothing wrong with realising a real tangible cash profit.

# 10

# Investing is not a process of perfect

*Shareplicity 2* has covered a lot of terrain. Understanding US stock markets is by no means easy. However, in this book I hope you find strategies and pathways that will help to break down what may, at first, seem a complex and overwhelming task.

We started the journey looking at the 'macro' picture, examining how the US financial system has evolved over the last 50 years and what is possibly in store for the future. Of course, no one knows the future. However, as stock markets are forward-looking, we devote considerable words and analysis to evolving frameworks for the future. Even if you are unsure of the future, a greater understanding of what *could* happen will help you make better risk-adjusted investment decisions that suit your age, savings goals and time frames.

The world of investing in US stocks has changed considerably from even 10 years ago. Therefore, I have aimed to provide some depth and scope about how the stock markets are different, and whether we may be on the verge of one of the most bullish decades in a generation.

After we explored the intricacies of US monetary policy, and the 'financialisation' of the markets, we started putting together the pieces of the stock puzzle.

*Shareplicity 2* approached the thorny topic of valuing the US stock giants – which highlighted how divergent valuations can be – against the macro-economic backdrop. As we moved through the chapters, the impact of interest rates and the cost of finance became clearer and their influence on the stock narratives more pronounced.

## It's not just about the numbers

One thing that I hope you have learned is that investing in stocks is never a binary decision. It is neither a complete science nor a complete art, but a wonderful blend of the two.

There are many books on how you can calculate value and there are programmes for buying and selling stocks which evaluate companies on a purely numerical basis.

As you have learnt, Shareplicity is not an advocate of the numerical depiction of a stock being the one and only deciding factor on whether to buy or sell. Stocks are just a price, and a price does not absolutely reflect the company, which is an underlying, complex ecosystem of humanity and, increasingly, automation – with many externalities and input factors. And, don't forget, great leaders have the capacity to create great companies and winning stock investments too.

I want you to take away from *Shareplicity 2* that picking the game-changing wealth-makers will not always be how you envisaged buying a stock. It may not be the well-known names you know, but a relative newcomer that is changing the world in terms of the technology we use.

Investors need an open mind, the ability to change their mind, and to be receptive to the idea that the world for now has irrevocably changed. I don't mean just since the COVID pandemic, but due to the interventionist policies of the Federal Reserve and, by default, other central banks, as the world for now is tied to and influenced by the US dollar and the US stock markets.

You have gone on a quick journey in *Shareplicity 2*, which I hope has at the very least opened your eyes to new ideas and concepts, no matter how obtuse and unrealistic they may seem in the 2021.

If someone were to ask me what has been one of the biggest successes of my life, I would say it has been the ability to adapt and change. Resilience, and the ability to know when you are wrong, be humble and accept errors and move on, are all important.

It may seem odd to you, but investing in stocks and great companies is a bit like life's journey. Nothing is set in stone and nothing lasts forever. But, you can find what works for you and what will make your investing journey successful.

For those of you who have ever attempted to master the game of golf, you will know exactly what I am saying. Investing, like golf, is 'not a game of perfect' (with a nod to the title of the bestselling book by Bob Cullen and Bob Rotella).

It is important to point this out, as investing is as much about managing risk as picking the best stock idea or narrative. As in golf, when you cannot always bomb the ball down the fairway in search of the elusive eagle (two shots under par), you can't go for broke investing heavily in one stock, because it may just leave you just that – broke.

I know there are many traders who look to charts and patterns, and there are momentum investors who follow the trend, but we are all individuals and finding the right pathways for our risk tolerance is a journey. There is nothing wrong with starting small and developing some confidence as you go. Try to seek out the best information sources and, if in doubt, you can always fall back on the steady-as-she-goes ETF products as a way to diversify.

Shareplicity remains a strong advocate for investing in new or existing quality companies within long-term secular growth trends. Around that theme, there is scope to add more value growth or value that also exhibits the ability to adapt and change.

How fortunate are we all now to have the opportunity to invest in great companies and stock markets overseas?

For the large part, the technological disruption and innovation of the internet has allowed for the democratisation of investing. Hopefully, more of you will be able to start on your own investment journey, because I believe the next ten years will be a golden period for stock investing. Nowhere else can you gain exposure to such an investment opportunity than via the largest, and some of the most liquid and regulated, markets in the world.

If investing directly in US stock markets is not for you, then the opportunities will continue to evolve in your own home country. Although Australia's US offering may seem small by international comparisons, the size and choice of new investing opportunities is growing by the day.

There are some major challenges ahead for the world on many fronts but the great companies will embrace the challenges and create opportunities along the way.

Remember, don't bite off more than you can chew. You don't have to be part of every new trend or fad. Stay focused on the quality stocks with strong tailwinds of growth and changing consumer habits.

Don't underestimate the new investors from differing demographics who will bring new eyes to the stocks. Millennials and the gen Z investors do not necessarily want to invest like their parents or grandparents and what is inconceivable to one demographic is a no-brainer to another.

## There's no right or wrong

It is wrong to dismiss a stock either as wrong or right. However, if a stock like Tesla has given the world of investing one important lesson, then it's that the so-called experts have been either late to the party or didn't show up at all. The new breed of Tesla followers have created incomes for themselves through innovative and informative social media platforms that analyse the company 24/7, 52 weeks of the year.

A market will always be made up of by bipolar opposites, and this is reflected in opinions of Tesla. Only time will tell whether the stock is just part of a trendy speculative bubble (after all, just how many years of forward earnings can be discounted into the stock price?), or if the holy grail of fully autonomous driving software transfers the company into the most vertically integrated hardware and software-as-a-service energy and mobility giant on earth.

I know where the young investors stand and, from where I am writing, it is their future and their money and savings that have the potential to change the world.

You also need to acknowledge where your biases may lie. Your unconscious streams of thought will play out in the way in which you view stocks and the US stock markets. I for one am progressive in nature and thrive off change. Some of you are likely to seek shelter in what you know. Neither approach is right or wrong, as long as you can keep your eyes open to the alternatives.

Defining your personal risk tolerance and how you mix and match your stock portfolios are also important. As we are living longer, our savings are having to work harder for us to obtain the returns we want later in life or to help our families.

If you are young, I hope that you will have the money-making opportunities afforded to the generations that have come before you. There is not a day when I don't recognise how fortunate I have personally been to have lived and worked through some of the biggest bull markets in history.

I have also experienced visceral fear when stock markets have crashed. But you cannot invest with that fear as, by and large, the system has worked and kept working for decades.

## Investing with purpose

You now also have the opportunity to invest your money with purpose. If 2020 taught me one thing, it was how ridiculously resilient human nature is when it comes to making money and finding creative pathways to problem-solving.

Investing in the next ten years will pose risks for those companies that do not adapt and adopt an ESG focus. With the largest investors in the world continuing to develop more prescriptive definitions of ESG metrics, those companies that choose to ignore the changes will ultimately pay the price of higher funding costs or, worse still, stranded, worthless assets.

What may be perceived as insurmountable risks by some are viewed as tremendous opportunities by others.

I do hope *Shareplicity 2* offers some insights into how the world's largest stock markets operate and the opportunities they offer.

This decade will be truly seminal, and riding the tsunami of quality change-making stocks may change your life in more ways than you could have ever imagined.

Dream big, think big and keep your eyes wide open!

# About the author

Danielle Ecuyer pursued a successful career for 15 years in institutional equities stockbroking and wealth management after completing her Commerce degree at the University of New South Wales. She trained and worked as an Australian equities analyst for BZW Australia in Sydney, consolidating her knowledge of fundamental share analysis. In 1990, Danielle moved to London to work in institutional equities sales in global emerging markets and specialised wealth management. Here she was employed in senior positions at some of the world's pre-eminent financial firms in the 1990s and looked after some of the world's largest emerging market investors in a time of great change.

After retiring, Danielle became a full-time investor while raising her son, working for NGOs and pursuing other passions. With over four decades of successful domestic and international experience in share investing in both a professional and personal capacity, Danielle drew on her wealth of expertise and wisdom to write *Shareplicity: a simple approach to share investing*. Released during the global pandemic, *Shareplicity* quickly hit the bestsellers lists and stayed there for most of the year.

*Shareplicity 2* is a response to calls for more information on gaining wider exposure to stocks on the US markets.

Danielle's experiences of the investment world as an adviser and client allow her to bring a fresh and independent perspective to share investing. *Shareplicity 2* aims to educate and inform both new and existing investors, challenge traditional views using extensive research from global expert commentators, and provide up-to-date data and information about what is happening in stock markets and 21st-century investment themes.

It's one thing to have a couple of good years of investing under your belt, yet another to survive and succeed over the long term. This was Danielle's goal and one she has achieved. And you can too.

# Resources and further reading

## Chapter 1

The Motley Fool, Tesla (TSLA) Q3 2020 Earnings Call Transcript, https://www.fool.com/earnings/call-transcripts/2020/10/22/tesla-tsla-q3-2020-earnings-call-transcript/

## Chapter 2

Carville, James https://www.bloomberg.com/news/articles/2018-01-29/the-daily-prophet-carville-was-right-about-the-bond-market-jd0q9r1w

MSCI emerging markets index msci.com/our-solutions/index/emerging-markets.

Nasdaq.com https://www.nasdaq.com/articles/when-performance-matters%3A-nasdaq-100-vs.-sp-500-2020-04-24 and nasdaq.com/market-activity/quotes/nasdaq-ndx-index.

Sector indices https://www.spglobal.com/spdji/en/documents/additional-material/sp-sector-indices.pdfwww.spglobal.com

## Chapter 3

CrossBorder Capital, 'Liquidity capital flows and how they affect the investment outlook and conclusions'

Federal Reserve Bank of St Louis https://www.stlouisfed.org/publications/regional-economist/january-2005/volckers-handling-of-the-great-inflation-taught-us-much

Hoisington Investment Management Company https://hoisington.com/pdf/HIM2020Q3NP.pdf

Howells, Michael https://www.realvision.com/shows/live/videos/rip-van-winkle-liquidity-edition-live-with-michael-howell

Lewis, Michael, 2015 *The Big Short – Inside the Doomsday Machine*, W.W. Norton & Company

Shvets, Viktor, 2020 *The Great Rupture, Three Empires, Four Turning Points, and the Future of Humanity*, Boyle & Dalton

Statista https://www.statista.com/statistics/248004/percentage-added-to-the-us-gdp-by-industry/

## Chapter 4

Retail sales in the US:

- https://www.digitalcommerce360.com/2020/11/17/walmarts-ecommerce-sales-jump-79-in-fiscal-q3/#:~:text=2020%20Top%201000%20Report&text=U.S.%20ecommerce%20sales%20for%20Walmart,fiscal%202021%2C%20which%20ended%20Oct.&text=Ecommerce%20sales%20contributed%20about%20570,comparable%20sales%20growth%2C%20Walmart%20reported

- https://www.digitalcommerce360.com/article/quarterly-online-sales/

Exxon Mobil: https://corporate.exxonmobil.com/News/Newsroom/News-releases/2020/1130_ExxonMobil-to-prioritize-capital-investments-on-high-value-assets

## Chapter 5

Bessembinder, Prof Hendrik's 'Do stocks outperform Treasury bills?' https://wpcarey.asu.edu/department-finance/faculty-research/do-stocks-outperform-treasury-bills

Callinan, James L., Osterweis Capital Management https://www.osterweis.com/insights/cyclical_vs_secular

Fisher, Philip A,. 2003 *Common Stocks and Uncommon Profits*, Wiley

Galloway, Prof Scott https://www.businessinsider.com/scott-galloway-robinhood-fueling-bubble-tesla-overvalued-2020-10?r=AU&IR=T

Kindig, Beth https://beth.technology/podcast-with-motley-fool-im-bullish-on-these-trends-for-2021/

Krom, Bradley https://www.wisdomtree.com/blog/2015-04-02/why-are-u-s-treasury-bonds-trading-like-growth-stocks

Martin, Laura https://www.cnbc.com/2021/01/28/heres-what-major-wall-street-analysts-had-to-say-about-apples-earnings-report.html

Munger, Charlie https://www.youtube.com/watch?v=sJxasvfUEJQ

Shvets, Viktor, 2020 *The Great Rupture, Three Empires, Four Turning Points, and the Future of Humanity*, Boyle & Dalton

Stevens, Louis A. https://www.thedigitalreport.com/roku-the-future-of-tv-operating-systems-nasdaqroku-seeking-alpha/

## Chapter 6

ARK Invest https://twitter.com/arkinvest/status/13145626751 92496129lang=en

ARK Invest, 'Big Ideas 2021', p.31. https://ark-invest.com/ big-ideas-2021/

ARK Invest, Software-As-A-Service | Could 2020-2030 be the Golden Age https://research.ark-invest.com/hubfs/1_Download_ Files_ARK-Invest/White_Papers/ARKInvest_070520_ Whitepaper_SaaS.pdf?hsCtaTracking=fab690aa-f254-460d-956b-a0cc1f233d4e%7C00f562bb-cead-43e1-9faf-6572010034cf

Barra, Mary https://media.gm.com/media/us/en/gm/news.detail.html/ content/Pages/news/us/en/2020/nov/1119-electric-portfolio.html

Bezos, Jeff https://blog.aboutamazon.com.au/amazon-in-australia/ email-from-jeff-bezos-to-employee

BMC blog, SaaS in 2021: Growth Trends & Statistics https://www. bmc.com/blogs/saas-growth-trends/

Carney, Mark https://www.ft.com/content/e5b57ece-0c31-4f42-9229-c8981bc9fd34

Cowen Research Themes 2021 https://www.cowen.com/insights/ themes-2021/

Dimon, Jamie https://www.cnbc.com/2021/01/15/jamie-dimon-says-jpmorgan-chase-should-absolutely-be-scared-s-less-about-fintech-threat.html

Fink, Larry https://www.blackrock.com/corporate/investor-relations/ larry-fink-ceo-letter

https://www.barrons.com/articles/why-draftkings-stock-could-more-than-double-51605631230

Kindig, Beth https://twitter.com/beth_kindig/status/135267377 6090025985Cowen Research Themes 2021 – I https://www.cowen. com/insights/themes-2021/

McKinsey Global Institute, A Future that Works: Automation, Employment, and Productivity https://www.mckinsey.com/~/media/ mckinsey/featured%20insights/Digital%20Disruption/Harnessing %20automation%20for%20a%20future%20that%20works/MGI-A-future-that-works-Executive-summary.ashx

Montgomery, Roger https://rogermontgomery.com/disruptive-innovations-are-evolutionary-not-revolutionary-part-i/

Werner, Tom https://www.cnbc.com/video/2021/01/08/sunpower-ceo-says-the-future-is-bright-for-renewable-energy-during-bidens-administration.html?&qsearchterm=Tom%20Werner%20sunpower

Wood, Cathie, ARK Invest https://research.ark-invest.com/hubfs/1_Download_Files_ARK-Invest/White_Papers/ArkInvest_101420_Whitepaper_BadIdeas2020.pdf

## Chapter 7

Ark Invest funds https://www.nasdaq.com/articles/ark-invest-etfs-power-active-investing-growth-2021-02-09

*Australian Financial Review* https://www.afr.com/markets/equity-markets/kiwi-energy-players-brace-for-blackrock-etfs-mega-selldown-20210402-p57g8n

Hyperchange https://podcasts.apple.com/al/podcast/warren-buffett-buys-chevron/id1272398195?i=1000509735684 https://www.ft.com/content/9e3e1d8b-bf9f-4d8c-baee-0b25c3113319

PRI https://www.unpri.org/investment-tools/an-introduction-to-responsible-investment

Statista https://www.statista.com/statistics/350525/number-etfs-usa/

## Chapter 8

A Wealth of Common Sense https://awealthofcommonsense.com/2021/02/a-short-history-of-u-s-stock-market-corrections-bear-markets/

Mordor Intelligence https://www.mordorintelligence.com/industry-reports/smartphones-market

Morgan Stanley, The Math of Value and Growth https://www.morganstanley.com/im/publication/insights/articles/article_themathofvalueandgrowth_us.pdf

Piper Sandler's Spring 2021, Taking Stock with Teens® survey https://www.pipersandler.com/1col.aspx?id=6216

## Chapter 9

Collapse of Archegos https://www.bloomberg.com/news/articles/2021-03-30/a-glossary-to-understand-the-collapse-of-archegos-quicktake?sref=t3Amjil0

GameStop https://edition.cnn.com/2021/02/25/investing/stock-settlement-period-robinhood-gamestop/index.html

Investopedia https://einvestingforbeginners.com/dcf-valuation/)

Liquidity Cascades https://www.thinknewfound.com/liquidity-cascades

Medcraft, Greg, February 19, 2020 Saturday Extra, ABC RN.

Wood, Cathie https://twitter.com/cathiedwood/status/1233357646608158720

## Chapter 10

Cullen, Bob and Rotella, R. *Not a game of perfect.* https://www.google.com/search?client=safari&rls=en&q=golf+is+not+a+game+of+perfect&ie=UTF-8&oe=UTF-8

# Acronyms and abbreviations

| | |
|---|---|
| ADR | American Depository Receipts |
| AI | Artificial intelligence |
| AOFM | Australian Office of Financial Management |
| CAGR | Compound average growth rate |
| CBOE | Chicago Board Options Exchange |
| CPI | Consumer price index |
| DCF | Discounted cash flow |
| DJIA | Dow Jones Industrial Average |
| EBITDA | Earnings before interest, tax and depreciation or amortisation |
| ESG | Environmental, social, governance |
| ETF | Exchange traded fund |
| EV | Electric vehicle |
| EV-to-sales | Enterprise-value-to-sales |
| FAANMG | Facebook, Apple, Amazon, Netflix, Microsoft and Google |
| FOMO | Fear of missing out |
| FSD | Full self-driving |
| GARP | Growth at a reasonable price |

| | |
|---|---|
| GDP | Gross domestic product |
| HFT | High frequency trading |
| IaaS | Infrastructure-as-a-service |
| ICE | Internal combustion engine |
| ICMA | International Capital Market Association |
| IPO | Initial public offering |
| MSCI | Morgan Stanley Country Index |
| NYSE | New York Stock Exchange |
| OTC | Over the counter (trades) |
| PaaS | Platform-as-a-service |
| PER | Price-to-earnings ratio |
| QE | Quantitative easing |
| RBA | Reserve Bank of Australia |
| S&P | Standard & Poor's |
| SaaS | Software-as-a-service |
| SEC | Securities and Exchange Commission |
| SPACs | Special purpose acquisition companies |
| SVOD | Subscription video on demand |
| TAM | Total addressable market |
| TIPs | Treasury inflation protected securities |
| yoy | Year-on-year |

# Glossary of financial terms

**Assets under management (AUM).** The total market value of assets held in a fund, such as a real estate investment trust.

**Capital expenditure (capex).** Money invested by a company in plant and equipment which is carried as assets on the balance sheet.

**Compound annual growth rate (CAGR).** The annual growth rate of an investment over time, including reinvesting the profits, usually expressed as a percentage.

**Compounding.** When the interest on the principal or the dividend income on shares is reinvested in the original amount to increase the total returns over time.

**Corporate bonds.** Instead of shares, companies can issue corporate bonds (to raise money) as a debt instrument that has defined characteristics depending on the issue (duration and interest paid). Corporate bonds rate higher than shares if a company is wound up.

**Dividend (also known as distribution).** This is the money shareholders 'earn' from holding a share. In Australia, dividends are usually paid twice a year from the profits made by the company they have invested in. Dividends are paid quarterly in the US.

**Dividend per share (DPS).** The amount of cash or equivalent paid to each shareholder out of the earnings per share.

**Dividend yield.** In simple terms, this is the amount shareholders earn from their investment by way of a dividend or distribution. It's calculated as the annual dividend per share divided by the share price, expressed as a percentage per annum. Historical yield is last year's dividend over today's share price, forward yield is forecast dividend over today's share price, and the yield achieved by a shareholder is the dividend divided by the price of entry into the stock.

**Earnings before interest and tax (EBIT).** A company's profits in a defined period before deducting interest charges and tax.

**Earnings before interest, tax, depreciation and amortisation (EBITDA).** A company's profits in a defined period before deducting interest charges, tax, depreciation and amortisation.

**Earnings per share (EPS).** A listed company's net profit for a period divided by the number of shares outstanding (held by investors) on the stock exchange.

**Emerging markets.** Markets of countries that are evolving to more mature economies. They are typified by lower levels of income and less development and industrialisation, but are developing into more affluent and modern economies.

**Exchange traded fund (ETF).** A low-cost passive or active listed fund that can represents a share index, a sector, currencies or bonds or a group of financial securities (stocks) that are defined by a theme or stated mandate.

**Ex-dividend date.** The date which is the cut-off for shareholders to be entitled to receive the dividend.

**Financialisation.** Refers to the increasing importance of financial assets and services, financial markets and financial institutions to an economy's GDP.

**Financial year (FY).** The 12-month period over which a company accounts for its business. The financial year varies between countries.

**Funds under management (FUM).** The total market value of funds being managed by a fund manager.

**Gross domestic product (GDP).** The total monetary value of goods and services produced by a country, usually over a year.

**Inflation.** The term for the rise in prices of goods and services over time.

**Initial public offering (IPO).** When a company lists its shares for the first time on the share market (also referred to as a 'float' or 'listing').

**Institutional investors.** Funds, superannuation funds, companies and banks that invest at scale in the stock market.

**Listed investment company (LIC).** Similar to a LIT, except it has shares (not units) listed on the stock exchange and the company status allows it to manage how it pays out the dividends and franking credits. That is, unlike for a LIT, all the dividend payments don't have to be distributed each year: they can be carried over and the income streams smoothed over time. The shares can trade at a discount or premium to the net tangible assets/net asset value, depending on shareholder demand.

**Listed investment trust (LIT).** A closed fund that has a fixed number of units available to buy on the stock exchange. The fund invests in shares and the shareholder receives the dividend income. Often LITs trade at a discount to the net asset value, meaning the share price doesn't fully reflect the value of the trust.

**Market capitalisation** or 'market cap' (sometimes simply called 'capitalisation'). The value of a stock implied by the current share price multiplied by the number of ordinary shares on issue.

**Net profit after tax (NPAT).** An accounting term that measures for a company how much profit is left after the costs of operating the business have been deducted.

**Net tangible assets (NTA).** Today's value of a company's tangible assets (such as buildings), not intangible assets (such as goodwill). An important measure for property trusts.

**Price-to-earnings ratio (PER)** (also referred to as P/E ratio). The current stock price of a company divided by past earnings (historical PER) or forecast earnings (forward PER) expressed as a multiple (for example, 10x).

**Quantitative easing (QE).** A monetary policy tool used by central banks to inject more liquidity into the financial system by purchasing financial securities (government and corporate bonds) from the market.

**Real estate investment trust (REIT).** A property fund listed on the stock exchange. Australian REITs are known as AREITs.

**Return on equity.** The percentage return annually on shareholders' funds. Net income divided by shareholders' equity.

**Rights issue.** When a company offers new shares to shareholders – usually at a discount to the existing share price – to raise equity (shareholders' funds).

**Secular market.** A market that's being driven by factors that underpin long-term growth in the market, unaffected by short-term trends.

**Share split.** When a company divides its shares into more shares and gives shareholders extra shares. As a result, each shareholder owns more shares but the total value remains the same.

**Total assessable market (TAM).** The total potential size of a new market that as yet has not been developed in terms of revenue and profits that can be generated from it over time.

**Treasury bonds.** Medium- to long-term, fixed interest rate financial instruments issued by governments to raise debt.

**Volatility.** Put simply, this is how much a share price or market goes up and down relative to the mean (average) or moving average share price.

# Index